Europe

Azores Islands

Canary Islands

Cape Verde

Africa

South America

THE TWO MOST
IMPORTANT VOYAGES OF
• AMERIGO VESPUCCI •

• ▸ • ▸ • ▸ THE SECOND FROM CADIZ, SPAIN
—→—→ THE THIRD FROM PORTUGAL

AMERIGO !

THE AMERIGO VESPUCCI STORY

By Frances Salter Nilsen and James Loring Salter

To Dorothy Brinkley
a good friend

Frances Salter Nilsen
February 1994

ii

Library of Congress Catalog Card Number: 92-093878
ISBN: 0-9633937-6-6
Bookland EAN: 9 780963 393760

First Edition
Printed in the United States of America

To Dr. J. W. Kerr
and his staff of
skilled caring nurses
Anne, Pauline, Dolly,
Kay, and others of
the Kingston General Hospital
Kingston, Ontario, Canada

Acknowledgments

I am grateful to the many people who helped me get the information and gave me the encouragement I needed to write this book. Special thanks to Mr. Tuggle, the research librarian at the Washington Library in Macon, Georgia. He and his staff were able to get the biographies of Amerigo through computer search from university libraries, Agnes Scott, Georgia Tech, and Murray College. The research librarians at Selby Library in Sarasota, Florida found a biography for me as did the librarians at Queens University in Kingston, Ont., Canada.

I want to especially thank my sister, Polly, and her son, Parks Hay for there continued support and encouragement. My children were helpful in many ways: Sarah gave me a computer and helped me learn to use it and also gave me much needed advice, Kirk, who gave me help in marketing the book, Marsha Conway Salter, who proof-read and helped design the cover, and James Loring Salter co-author, who was with me every step of the way, doing the typing, putting it on disk, and working with me on composition and spelling. His patience with me was remarkable.

PREFACE

Amerigo Vespucci was born in 1454, in a remarkable city and at a remarkable time. The time was the exciting 15th century and the city was Florence. It was in Florence, Italy, and at the time of the Medici that the great rebirth of art and learning known as the Renaissance began. The Medicis did much to encourage this revival in both art and learning and it reached its peak at the time of Lorenzo de Medici, known as Lorenzo, the Magnificent. Amerigo Vespucci was a contemporary of Lorenzo and it was he who established the Platonic Academy, the academy that his grandfather, Old Cosimo, had dreamed of establishing. He invited all the scholars, all the artists, all the writers, as well as wise older men, and eager young students to come together to study the old Greek and Roman manuscripts, to read poetry, and to exchange ideas. It was in this atmosphere that Amerigo grew up and it was in Florence that he spent the first 38 years of his life.

In his notebook when he was a student at the San Marco Monastery School, he wrote "I want to go, to see, and to know." And much of his life was spent going, seeing, and knowing. It was because of his knowledge that he was able to recognize South America as a new continent. He studied Latin and Greek but was more interested in astronomy and geography. His teacher and mentor was his uncle, Giorgio Antonio Vespucci, a well-known Florentine scholar and one of the first Florentines to embrace the philosophy of Humanism, the philosophy that emphasizes the dignity of man, his ability to reason, and his right to ask the question, "Why?"

Amerigo was fortunate to have lived in Florence during its Golden Age and he went to Seville in 1492, the year that marked the beginning of Spain's Golden Age. It was in this momentous year that Queen Isabella and King Ferdinand succeeded in driving the Moors back into Africa and gave Columbus permission to embark on his famous voyage.

Amerigo was in Seville when Columbus returned from this voyage and announced that he had found a western water route to India. There was much rejoicing. This voyage changed the geography of the world and ushered in a new era. A great fleet of seventeen vessels was ordered for Columbus's second voyage and Amerigo and his partner were commissioned to help outfit them. Later Amerigo also would make voyages to this new found land. He and Columbus at that time became friends and remained friends as long as they lived. Both wrote letters describing what they had discovered on their voyages. These letters were printed on the newly invented printing press and circulated all over Europe. They did much to inform the Europeans about the new discoveries. It is ironic that after their death they became the focus of a bitter controversy that has lasted for centuries.

Why was America named for Amerigo and not for Columbus was the subject of this great controversy. No one seemed to know exactly why. Both Columbus and Amerigo were in their graves long before it began. The true origin of the word AMERICA had been lost in the confusion of the times and it was believed by many early historians that Amerigo falsely claimed to be the discoverer. It was not until the early part of the 19th century that the true origin was finally known. It was unearthed by Alexander von Humboldt, the distinguished German explorer and naturalist. The letters Amerigo wrote telling about his voyages were also buried in the archives of Florence. One by one they, too, have been found and are shedding some light on this controversial question. This book is a novel telling the story of the early period of the exploration of America and the voyages made while Columbus was still alive. Samuel Eliot Morison, who was Columbus's biographer and America's most distinguished naval historian, terms them the "Minor Voyages" but they are important for they did much to explain what Columbus had discovered and to answer the question "Why was AMERICA named for Amerigo Vespucci and not for Columbus?" This novel explains why, as it tells Amerigo's story. Whether he deserved to have two continents named for him will not be argued, they were, and few Americans either in North America or in South America would want to change the name. AMERICA is a beautiful word. It just seems to be the right name for this land of freedom, and it has been said that "A successful name is a work of art."

Contents

xii

AMERIGO !

THE AMERIGO VESPUCCI STORY

By Frances Salter Nilsen and James Loring Salter

Chapter I

The Baptism of Amerigo

What if wise men, as far back as Ptolemy,

Judged that the earth like an orange was round:

None of them ever said, "Come along, follow me.

Sail to the West and the East will be found."

> Jingle written to celebrate the
> 400th Anniversary of the
> Discovery of America [1892]

It would be almost fifteen centuries after Ptolemy before a brave man would say, "Come along, follow me." That brave man was Christopher Columbus. With only a crude compass and the stars to guide him, he set sail into the unknown. He was the brave man who proved that by sailing "West the East could be found." It was

Columbus who led the way. It was Columbus who discovered America. Why, then, does it not bear his name? Why was America named for Amerigo Vespucci? To understand why we must go back in time to the fifteenth century. It is a long story. It began in 1454.

A little procession slowly made its way down the narrow and crooked streets of Florence, Italy. Its destination was to the famous Baptistery for the baptism of a special child. At that time no one but his family considered him special for it was only the customary baptism of any Florentine child in any influential Florentine family. This special child was Amerigo Vespucci, the man for whom two continents were named. He was the third son of Nastagio and Elisabetta Vespucci. Although his baptism was not the festive and joyous occasion of the first born, it was a serious procession that arrived at the Ghiberti doors of the Baptistery, the doors soon to be called "The Gates of Paradise" by Michelangelo. The child was in the arms of his grandfather, Old Amerigo Vespucci, for whom he was named.

The robed priest met them at the doors and asked, "What do you ask of the Church of God?"

"Faith," answered Old Amerigo for he was the godfather.

"And what does faith give you?" continued the priest?

"Life Everlasting," replied the old man.

"If you are to enter upon life everlasting, keep the commandment, you should love the Lord God with all your heart, with all your soul, with all your will, and love your neighbor as yourself." The priest then blew his breath on the child and made the sign of the cross three times, and ordered the devil to emerge from the child's body, saying, "Foul Spirit, come forth from him and yield place to the

Holy Spirit."

Then all prayed with the priest, "Per Christum Dominum nostrum. Amen." The priest then laid his hands on Amerigo's head and said, "God, all powerful and eternal, Father of our Lord, Jesus Christ, turn Thy glance on this Thy slave whom Thy hath deigned to initiate into the rudiments of the faith, remove all blindness from his heart; break all the chains of Satan that enslave him. Open to him the gates of Thy mercy so that signed with the seal of Thy wisdom, he may be free from evil desires and, drawn by the gentle perfume of Thy precepts, he may joyfully serve the Church and grow in virtue every day.

"Name this child," said the priest.

"Amerigo," answered his grandfather.

The priest then gave the infant a taste of the salt of wisdom. This caused a tiny whimper from him but little Amerigo soon followed the whimper with a smack of satisfaction at the new taste. The Priest then dipped his hands into the holy oil and anointed the child on the breast and back saying, "Amerigo, do you desire baptism?"

The godfather replied, "I do."

"Amerigo," continued the priest. I baptize you in the name of the Father, the Son, and the Holy Ghost. Go in peace, and may the Lord go with you."

All answered, "Amen."

Again the little procession made its way back through the "Gates of Paradise" onto the street toward the Vespucci home. At first they walked quietly for the baptismal rites had been impressive. "What would the future hold for the young child?" they wondered.

At last Guido Antonio spoke. Guido was the cousin of Nastagio and one of Amerigo's godfathers, "Did you notice that Amerigo smacked his lips at the taste of the salt? He quickly recognized it to be a new taste. No doubt, he will be quick of wit."

"And his eyes seemed to focus on the priest. That is unusual for a nine day old infant," joined in Giorgio Antonio, the child's uncle and another godfather.

Old Amerigo beamed with pride when he heard these observations and said, "No doubt, he will be a true Vespucci and do honor to our name, and no doubt he will be a worthy citizen of Florence."

Nastagio, the father, listened with pleasure to the words of the other three and just before they reached the great stone house, which was the Vespucci home, he said quietly, "It is important that all three of my sons have a good education and it is important that they become good citizens of Florence. It is my desire that they learn Greek and Latin from you, Giorgio, and you, Guido, will show them how to be good citizens of our beautiful city and instill in them a desire to serve it."

As they climbed the steps to the Vespucci home which was only a ten minute walk from the Baptistery, Old Amerigo stepped ahead of the others and paused before the Vespucci coat of arms. He bade the others listen, "I am old," he said, "It is not likely that I will live long enough to fulfill the promises made in the church today in Amerigo's behalf. I charge you three with the responsibility for carrying out those vows."

"We promise," said the three gentlemen and all looked solemnly at the Vespucci coat of arms, a bright red shield with a blue border, on which was painted a golden wasp.

"The wasp is an industrious insect and the Vespucci have always been doers. Amerigo must be taught to follow Christ, to be a serious thinker, a careful worker, and then I am sure he will be a worthy citizen of Florence. It will largely be your responsibility to be sure that he is, if you fail this Old Vespucci wasp will rise from his grave and sting you." Old Amerigo continued half seriously and half jokingly, and the three men promised even as they smiled.

This coat of arms had been conferred upon the Vespucci family many generations before by the Duke of Tuscany. The name, Vespucci, means wasp in Italian.

Nastagio opened the heavy door and the group entered. Many guests had assembled to take part in the festivities.

Elisabetta, the child's mother, called from an adjoining room where she was resting on a couch. "Did the baptism go well? Did Amerigo behave himself? Bring him to me for he must be hungry."

Nastagio promptly took the baby from his grandfather's arms and carried him to his mother. "He behaved well, he only gave a slight whimper when the priest touched his tongue with salt. Then he quickly smacked his lips. You can be proud of him."

The infant snuggled down beside his mother and with another smack took hold of the waiting breast.

Amerigo's older brother, Antonio, who was only three, ran to the bedside. Girolamo, the other brother toddled along after him.

They watched with interest as Amerigo ate his lunch.

Antonio would grow up to be a lawyer and later a priori to the Signoria in Florence, like his father, as the eldest son is expected to do. Girolamo, as was the custom for the second son, would enter the church and become a monk. What was in store for Amerigo was the big topic of the evening.

"I predict that Amerigo will become a great teacher," said his uncle, Giorgio Antonio, who was a monk and a teacher in the nearby San Marco Monastery School. "No doubt, but that he will become a great Greek scholar and translate many Greek manuscripts. There is so much ancient knowledge just waiting to be rediscovered."

"The Greeks had the best ideas for government," joined in Guido Antonio, the other godfather. I predict that Amerigo will become a great statesman like Plato and Socrates and serve our city well.

"And may he, like Socrates, be a worthy citizen of his city. Florence needs such statesmen," added old Amerigo. "May he be worthy of the Vespucci name."

Chapter II

Peretola

It was the year 1457. Three years had passed since Amerigo's baptism. Two more processions had made their way to the Baptistery for the baptism of two more Vespucci children, Bernardo, another son, and Agnoletta, a beautiful baby girl. She was to be the last of Nastagio and Elisabetta's children.

Many generations ago the Vespucci family had moved to Florence but they had originated in the village of Peretola, which was a short distance outside Florence. Peretola, like Florence was in the Tuscany region, the region that had been the home of the early Etruscans. Amerigo was proud to be a Tuscan. The family was descended from Count Soliciano who lived in Peretola in the 13th century. The Vespucci family was probably the most distinguished family that Peretola produced and later a stone was placed inscribed as follows: "In this village of Peretola the noble and powerful family of the Vespucci had its origin, one of whose sons was the great Amerigo from whom America got its name."

There were other distinguished members of the Vespucci family. One, Simone de Pero Vespucci acquired great wealth in the mercantile business. Three of the Vespucci had been chosen to be Gonfaloniere di Justice, the highest public office of Florence. Old Amerigo held that office for three terms. Twenty-five Vespucci held the office of Priori to the Signoria or Secretary of the Republic. That was the office held by Amerigo's father and later by his brother, Antonio.

Several of the Vespucci served as ambassadors for Florence and were influential in foreign affairs. Juliano Vespucci was ambassador to Geneva and Pistoria. Piero di Vespucci became ambassador to the King of Naples. He also had commanded a fleet of galleys in an attack on the Corsairs on the Barbary Coast.

Probably the most distinguished Vespucci would be Guido Antonio di Giovanni di Vespucci, the cousin of Nastagio and one of Amerigo's godfathers. He was a prominent lawyer as well as a man of letters. In the year of the Pazzi Conspiracy he was sent to France as ambassador and from the year 1480 until 1484, he served as Florence's ambassador to the Vatican. Ten years later he again served as ambassador to the French King Charles VIII. He was a priori for the Signoria several times and gonfaloniere, the chief executive of Florence, in 1497 and 1498. He had much influence on Amerigo's life.

It was Amerigo's, uncle, Giorgio Antonio, the brother of Nastagio, though, who had the most influence on his life. Giorgio was known in Florence for his learning and character. He was a scholar, a collector of manuscripts, and the owner of a splendid library. He was the priori of the San Marco Monastery School when Amerigo was a student there.

When the Vespucci moved within the walls of Florence, their

homes were located in the d'Ognissanti section, which was close to the city gate, Porta della Cana, later called Porta de Prato. The Vespucci houses were of stone. The most imposing one was that of the grandfather, Old Amerigo. It had frescoed walls, ceilings of great beams, and heavy oaken furniture. The Vespucci ate out of plates of majolica and silver. The house was built around an inner court with a large stone staircase to the second floor. It "presented a picture of comfort and elegance."

The home of Elisabetta and Nastagio was next door and was not so elegant but was a pleasant place for a growing family. The family all used the grandfather's home for special occasions.

Nearby was the home of Piero Vespucci. His son, Marcos, married the lovely Simonetta Callanes, a famous Florentine beauty, whose face was painted in many of Botticelli famous paintings. Simonetta was the same age as Amerigo and they were friends.

Ognissanti was the industrial quarter of the city. It was located at the junction of the Mugnone and Arno Rivers. The abundance of water made it ideal for tanning leather and for working in flax, straw, and wool. The Vespucci had a mill and were members of the powerful wool guild. Their neighbor, Mariano Filippi, was a tanner and had eight children. The youngest one, Alessandro Filippi, was to become the famous artist known as Botticelli. Botticelli, although a little older than Amerigo, was his contemporary and friend. In Ognissanti, a church was built by the friars, and a hospital by the Vespucci family. The Vespucci also built a chapel for the hospital. Paintings of the Vespucci family are in this chapel.

Although the Vespucci had moved into the city, they kept their country place in Peretola. It was left in the care of a cousin, but the family often spent weekends and holidays there. In contrast to the dirty and crowded streets of Florence, Peretola had green meadows and open sky. The air was fresh and there were always wild flowers and berries so the children were delighted when their father asked, "Who wants to go to Peretola?"

"I do! I do!" yelled the four boys in unison. Even little Agnoletta who was only a toddler would join in with "Me go! Me go!". The boys developed strong bodies by running across the meadows and fields. They played ball with the village children and later it was in Peretola that they learned to be expert horsemen.

Little Agnoletta was happy when she was chasing the barnyard fowls. "Duckie! Duckie!" was one of her first words. Her father, Nastagio, would sit on a bench and watch her with pride. Little Agnoletta had danced into the heart of all her family. Her brothers adored her, Elisabetta was pleased to have a little girl to dress in ribbons, ruffles, and lace, but little Agnoletta was especially dear to her father, Old Stagio. Nastagio, even while still young, came to be known as Old Stagio. It may have been because he was ten years older than his wife, Elisabetta, and Elisabetta never let him forget it. Contrary to the usual pattern, Elisabetta, or Mona Lisa, as the children called her (all Florentine children called their mother Mona Lisa) was the stern one and was often harsh with her husband and with her children. On the other hand, Old Stagio was mild and easy going.

Mona Lisa rarely went to Peretola with the family, "Peretola bores me," she declared. "I'll stay home for some peace and quiet." As the years went by Old Stagio and the children went more often, perhaps to escape Mona Lisa's sharp tongue, and also so the children could have room to romp and play.

It was on these visits to Peretola that Amerigo first became interested in the heavens. He lay on his back in the cool summer grass and watched the clouds in the daytime and the stars at night. Often the Italian sky is cloudless and at night the stars were particularly brilliant in Peretola away from the smoke of the crowded city. Often Amerigo would be accompanied by his Uncle Giorgio. Together, they would lie on the grass at twilight and watch the stars appear. They also observed the sun at different seasons of the year and observed the movement of the clouds by the wind. Soon all the constellations and their location at all times of the year were familiar to them.

Uncle Giorgio had studied astronomy and was an excellent teacher, and Amerigo was an eager student. Later Amerigo, too, would become a student of astronomy at the San Marco School. His brothers teased him about always having "his head in the clouds." He just shrugged off the teasing and continued his pastime while at Peretola and continued this interest for all the rest of his life.

He often would take little Agnoletta for a short walk at the twilight hour and together they would watch the stars pop out. "That is Venus," he would tell her. "Venus is the most beautiful star of all."

Sometimes little Agnoletta would cry out in glee, "Venus, Venus!" even before he pointed it out. She would laugh in delight when a rainbow appeared in the sky and picking the wild flowers in the meadow also delighted her. "I will take these to Mona Lisa," she would say.

Possibly, however, her greatest joy was in blowing soap bubbles, and like a soap bubble she had floated into the household and had brought to it all the warmth and color of the rainbow. Her brothers quarreled less in her presence. They did not like to see her distressed. Her father, Old Stagio, who often enjoyed a night of revelry with his friends, came home more often, and even Mona Lisa's tongue was not so sharp.

Agnoletta, though, like the soap bubbles she so delighted in, was soon to vanish. She had always been a delicate child. Even in the daytime she would often climb into her mother's lap to rest and by evening she was exhausted. Then she would climb into Old Stagio's lap and he would rock her gently back and forth until she fell asleep.

Both Mona Lisa and Old Stagio soon became worried about her and called in a doctor. The doctor said, "She seems to be developing consumption like her cousin, Simonetta. We will have to watch her carefully."

This news spread gloom on the Vespucci household for at that time there was no cure for consumption. It also brought a period of peace and quiet to the household for all sought to keep the little girl happy. The boys quarreled even less and the sharp exchanges between their parents almost ceased.

They went to Peretola more often for there she got more fresh air and fresh milk. For a brief time, the treatment seemed to be helping, and again she danced about among the geese and ducks. The family became hopeful, "She is going to get well," they whispered to each other.

Soon, however, little Agnoletta was again pale and wan. She always sought someone's arms to hold her tight when her little body was racked with spells of coughing. Soon she was too weak even to hold up her head. Either her father, her mother, or one of her brothers stayed with her both day and night.

One night she took a turn for the worst. The doctor was summoned, but she was beyond his help.

The anxious parents were upstairs at her bedside while the boys waited anxiously below. Hours passed. They hardly dared move and when they spoke, it was in hushed tones so as not to disturb the little sick girl. Suddenly the boys heard their mother cry out, "Oh Stagio, she IS gone."

Old Stagio came slowly down the steps and gathered the boys around him, "An angel has come to take our little Agnoletta to heaven. She will be with God and Christ," he said huskily.

This was the boys' first experience with death. They clung to their father and wept.

"We must not be sad," said Old Stagio. "She was needed in heaven, God just loaned her to us for a little while. Her place is with the angels and we can be glad that she will never have to cough again." The latter was said as much to comfort himself as well as the boys.

"How is Mona Lisa?" the boys asked.

"She will be all right," Old Stagio replied, "But now I must return to her. You boys, get undressed and ready for bed."

The boys, however, continued to weep. The tears flowed as if they would never stop. Finally, young Antonio choked back his tears long enough to remind the others "As father says, Little Agnoletta is with the angels. She will like that."

"And she was like a little angel on earth," sobbed Girolamo.

"Yes," joined in Amerigo, "and to me she was a twinkling little star. Every night when the stars are out, I will think of her."

Young Girolamo put his arms around the bewildered little Bernardo and whispered, "I will never tease you any more, Bernardo. Agnoletta did not like that."

"We must all be better in every way for she would want it that way," said Antonio firmly.

"I will be good for 'Lette'," young Bernardo sobbed.

Upstairs Old Stagio, who probably would feel the loss more keenly than the rest, attempted to console his grieving wife. "Think of our little Agnoletta skipping and dancing in heaven. We must be thankful that she will no longer be racked with pain ___ and you, my Elisabetta, are now the mother of an angel."

At that Elisabetta who had been stiffly sitting beside the dead child, turned to her husband and sought the comfort of his arms.

"And you, Stagio, are so good. You are a good father and husband." And indeed the death of the little girl brought the whole family closer together.

"We will always miss our little Agnoletta, but we were blessed to have her for a little while," stated Old Stagio firmly. He took his wife's arm and they continued to cling to each other's hand as they walked down the stairs to comfort their boys.

Chapter III

His Schooling

It was the year 1469. Amerigo was almost sixteen years old and was a student at the San Marco Monastery School. San Marco was the school for the sons of the noble and wealthy families of Florence. Amerigo's older brothers, Antonio and Girolamo had been students there but now they were continuing their studies in the University of Pisa.

Giorgio Antonio Vespucci, Amerigo's uncle and godparent, who was the priori or headmaster of the school, was a well known scholar. He studied Greek and Latin but was particularly interested in the sciences. He became one of the great humanists of his day, and taught Amerigo to seek rational explanation for all things. Giorgio also had a great hatred for tyranny in government and a great thirst for justice. The injustices he saw all around him made him sad.

In the San Marco School both religious and secular values intermingled. It was here at San Marco that the Greek scholars translated the old manuscripts. They were first brought to Florence by

Old Cosimo de Medici, who during his seventy-five years at the helm in Florence had commissioned Marselo Ficini to translate the works of Plato from the Greek. Cosimo made San Marco the repository for the six hundred books he had collected. This was the beginning of the first public library for these six hundred books became the core of Florence's famous Biblioteca Laurenziana.

It was here at San Marco, because of this library and because of the teaching of Giorgio, that Amerigo received the well-rounded education that enabled him to recognize that part of the land Columbus had discovered was a new continent and not Asia.

It was here that Amerigo and Piero Soderini became friends, a friendship that would continue throughout their life. The Soderini family like the Vespucci and Medici families was among the most influential and wealthy of Florence. Both Amerigo and Piero were serious students. Both studied Greek and Latin, astronomy and geography. Amerigo preferred astronomy and geography while Piero was more interested in Greek, especially Plato's Republic. Both remained at the San Marco School to pursue their studies under the guidance of the scholar, Giorgio.

The school day at San Marco was long and varied, for the Florentines were serious about the education of their youth. There were free schools for the poor and girls were also educated. Many girls became Latin and Greek scholars. The school day at all schools began at an early hour with morning prayer. They then read their lessons until the noon Mass. After Mass came lunch and a period of relaxation. Then, since Florence's economy depended on industry and trade, the students were taken by a Master's assistant to visit the places of trade and industry. The older students would later become apprentices and remain for four hours at the trade or industry of their choice. Since Amerigo was to enter the banking and mercantile business, his apprenticeship was in a bank. The younger students after their visit to the trade centers would be given an hour to run and play before returning to their lessons. A mid-afternoon snack would follow the study hours. After that the student would take fencing or dancing lessons. Then they returned to the classroom for an hour of study. The day students would return home after the study hour. The boarding students would dine at seven and then go "to music" or whatever their talent "seem to indicate" until bedtime.

The Florentines were also serious about their festivals and holidays. They celebrated ninety-six holidays yearly besides their own special occasions. A very special occasion was soon to be celebrated. It would mark both Lorenzo de Medici's wedding to Clarice Orsini of Rome and his twenty-first birthday. Piero, Lorenzo's father, had just died and Lorenzo had inherited the political power of Florence so this would be a great time of celebration in the city.

It was just before this big event that San Marco was honored by a visit from Lorenzo. The purpose of his visit was to encourage learning and the arts. He told the boys in a stirring speech that the continued greatness of Florence depended on the type of education that they received. He concluded by asking Uncle Giorgio to choose his top students to be torchbearers in his coming celebration. It was a day both Amerigo and Piero would always remember because they were among those selected.

After Lorenzo's inspiring speech and his departure, Giorgio quieted the boys down and wrote the following assignment on the board:

Copy and memorize the following quotations in both Latin and Italian.

Hate Evil Governments
Be Honest Always
Erudition without Morality
is worse than useless.

After such assignments Giorgio asked for comments and discussions. These quotations had an enduring effect on Amerigo's life. Often the discussion became quite lively. Today, Piero started off the discussion with a question, "What kind of government do we have in Florence?"

"It is a government of the people. Our ancestors long ago rejected the rule of the aristocracy," replied Amerigo. "No noble can hold office."

"True," agreed Giorgio, "but is it really rule by the people? It is estimated that 25% of the families have 65% of the eligibility for the Signoria. That leaves only 35% for the majority. Does that sound like rule by the people?"

"If that is true?" responded Piero, "We must seek to make the count more even. That is what you are suggesting, isn't it, Master Giorgio?"

"Yes," responded Giorgio, "the power does lie with the people but the people must assume it."

"But the Signoria does choose a new gonfaloniere every two months. That gives the power to change to the people, doesn't it?" joined in Amerigo.

"Yes and No," explained Giorgio, "For usually the gonfaloniere chosen is the one designated by the Medici. Old Cosimo de Medici only held the office of gonfaloniere for two months, but he directed the affairs of Florence for almost sixty years."

"Why was he allowed to do so?" questioned Piero.

"He guided the city wisely. He always had the best interest of Florence in mind when he made a decision," answered Giorgio.

"Is that why he was known as 'Pater Patriae?'" asked Amerigo.

"Yes," agreed Old Giorgio, "because for most of those years, Florence enjoyed peace and prosperity. All governments are more stable with a strong, wise, and unselfish leader. He was good for Florence."

"But Master Giorgio, you still try to instill in us the danger of dictatorship and harsh governments. It does seem that in our city, when a leader abuses his power, we have a way to change it."

"Let us hope so," retorted Giorgio, "but it is not easy to topple a ruthless dictator. Cosimo was good for Florence and Piero de Medici followed his father's example. Let us hope that Lorenzo also will prove to be as wise a leader. He's young for such a responsibility but the fact that he took time to visit us today to stress the value of education indicates that he probably will be. The people like him and since the power of a leader seems to depend on personal popularity, that will be in his favor."

Amerigo while at San Marco kept many notes in his exercise or copy book. This copy book is still extant and is kept in the Riccardi Library in Florence. Reading excerpts from it help explain Amerigo's actions in later life.

Of political life, Amerigo wrote in his book:

"Who are those few who have so grievously oppressed the many, and have spoiled what was theirs . . . which was great wealth . . . and which their oppressors prized and coveted? They were our fellow citizens, the friends of your family. They now depart to exile . . ."

Amerigo also wrote in this copy book:

"Oh, priest, to whom people so often turn for advice inquiring why lightning has struck, or hail, rain, or snow has fallen unseasonably as though you were the god Apollo, who as poets pretend can read the future as though it was the present, what would you reply to them if they were to ask you about the shower of stones, blood, and flesh so often mentioned in old fables?"

In another part of the book he writes, wondering about physiological facts, thus:

"What is the reason for men's blood to cool off? Why, at times does a man pale, or turn red, and again white, at times become bloated and then again gaunt . . . I have heard it said that the changes we undergo are caused by the actions of the blood, which is the beginning and the origin, the reason for our life."

Also the following passage was in the exercise book; this gives a reason for being in the mercantile business:

"Going back and forth to many lands, where by talking and trading one can learn many things, not a few merchants have become wise and learned, something that cannot be explained   in a few words.   Moving about and making inquiries concerning the world, whose limits we have not yet completely ascertained, they can furnish valuable advice by word and association to those who come to them in search of counsel or clarification of some doubts concerning matters of business and custom."

The Latin and Greek taught by Giorgio was not the dead language of the usual school masters. It was a living key that opened the door to science, to philosophy, and to the literature of the past. This kind of teaching bore some of the "finest fruits of thought which history records." Amerigo learned well under the tutelage of Giorgio while at San Marco and continued to seek his counsel in his adult life.

Chapter IV

Lorenzo, the Magnificent

It was the year 1470. The streets of Florence were decked out with banners and flowers for a great festival. The festival would be one of unusual splendor for it was the one being celebrated in honor of Lorenzo de Medici for both his twenty-first birthday and his marriage to Clarice Orsini of Rome. Lorenzo was now Florence's most important citizen for he had inherited the political power of Florence from his father who had died in December 1469. This political power had been held by Lorenzo's father, his grandfather, Cosimo di Medici, and even by a Medici before that. In fact, as Giorgio said, the Medici controlled Florence for most of the 15th and would continue for most of the 16th century. The great rebirth of learning known as the Renaissance began in Florence and was nurtured by Old Cosimo and reached its peak during Lorenzo's reign. This was the famous Quattrocento.

The festival to honor Lorenzo would begin with a colorful parade as was the custom and then be followed by a splendid tournament. In this tournament all the young men of Florence and of the surrounding area would show their skill in jousting and fencing.

The citizens of Florence were gathering, either to take part in the parade or to watch it. Among them were Amerigo and his friend, Piero Soderini. They were to be torch bearers. This was the parade in which they had been invited to participate by Lorenzo and it was the first time they had taken an active part in one. They were very excited for they would march right behind Lorenzo and his knights.

Clarice, the bride, was not in Florence for this festival. She would not arrive for four months. The marriage had been performed by proxy in Rome for pressing government affairs kept Lorenzo from leaving Florence. His cousin, Fillippi di Medici, stood in for him.

Amerigo and Piero watched as the gaily dressed participants took their places for the parade. Lorenzo was magnificently dressed for the occasion. He wore a handsome suit of armor that had been presented to him by the King of Naples. His surcoat worn over his armor was of white and purple velvet. His silk scarf and cape were embroidered with roses and pearls, and his black velvet cap was topped with a plume of golden threads. He rode a white charger draped in red and white velvet which, too, was embroidered in roses and pearls.

Even though Lorenzo was not a handsome man, he was a "striking figure" as he handed Lucrezia Donati into the waiting chariot. Lucrezia was the Queen of the tournament. She, too, was beautifully dressed in a silk robe embroidered with roses and pearls. She wore a crown encrusted with more pearls and other precious stones.

The boys watched admiringly, "Lucrezia is beautiful," said Piero. It is no wonder that Lorenzo is in love with her."

"Rumor had it that she, too, is in love with him but in spite of that she was betrothed and married to Bartholomew Donati," remarked Amerigo.

"Yes, but Lorenzo's marriage was arranged before her marriage," defended another torch bearer. "Even though the Donati family is one of the leading families in Florence, the Medici wanted a marriage for Lorenzo that would bring more prestige and political power to the city."

"Most Florentine marriages are arranged by the parents," commented Piero. "The brides' social position and the size of her dowry are the important considerations."

"Lorenzo's marriage to Clarice is considered very important for Florence," said Amerigo. "Uncle Giorgio says she brings a dowry of 6000 florins and that the Orsini family is one of the oldest and most powerful of Rome and Naples. The good will of such a family in these uncertain times is very important for Florence."

"Even before Lorenzo's father died his mother had been sent to Rome to arrange the marriage," added Piero. "It is said that Lorenzo has never seen his bride."

"I have heard that when he visited Rome he may have got a glimpse of her as she passed in a carriage," replied Amerigo. "I hope my family will never arrange a marriage for me."

"No wonder so many husbands have clandestine affairs," said Piero thoughtfully. "One can hardly blame them."

The parade was ready to begin. The fifers, the standard bearers, and the heralds blowing trumpets preceded Lucrezia's chariot.

Lorenzo and his handsomely decked out knights, all on spirited chargers, fell in behind the chariot. Amerigo and Piero, also handsomely dressed in silk shirts, velvet knee pants, and brightly colored stockings followed Lorenzo and his knights.

The parade proceeded down street after street of Florence until it reached the Piazza della Signoria which was the center of the town. There the tournament would be held. It was also gaily decorated with banners and flowers. This tournament, as with the usual tournaments of the 15th century, would not be the bloody affair of earlier times. It was mostly held to show off the skill and strength of the young men. As had been prearranged, Lorenzo was declared the winner and presented with the prize trophy.

The celebration was continued four months later when Clarice arrived from Rome. Four days of feasting and dancing celebrated this occasion. The great Medici Palace known as the Palazzo Vecchio was ablaze with light. In the great hall of the palace row after row of tables had been set up and, as was the custom of the time, men and women sat at different tables. The young women sat at Clarice's table, the young men at Lorenzo's, the older women sat at Lorenzo's mother's table, and the men of his father's generation dined in the courtyard.

What a merry time it was! The feasting lasted from twilight until almost midnight. Then the feasting was followed by dancing in the Piazzo. Only the elite of Florence were invited to the feasting but all the citizens of Florence were invited to the dance. Often strangers joined the merry crowd and the dancing lasted until the wee hours of the morning.

Amerigo and Piero had been asked to serve as pages for the banquet. Amerigo's job was to pour the wine and keep the wine coolers full. Piero was to pass the sweetmeats. They were kept busy for the crowd had had a long day.

"I believe this crowd has consumed three hundred barrels of wine," Amerigo declared to Piero as they passed each other in the courtyard. "This is a thirsty bunch."

"And I'm sure I've passed a thousand pounds of sweetmeats," was Piero's reply. "And as to the wine, you look like you, too, have consumed your share."

"Well, just a little," confessed Amerigo blushing.

As midnight approached the feasting ended and slowly the guests made their way to the piazza. Piero and Amerigo prepared to join them. "This will be a merry evening. Our townspeople drank like mad. I don't believe there is a sober one left," remarked Amerigo.

"And they ate like gluttons. Passing the sweetmeats turned out to be exhausting and I expected it to just be fun," complained Piero. "I'm bone tired."

"And so am I," agreed Amerigo as the two boys drifted out onto the piazza to join the dancers.

After a time Piero yawned and confessed to Amerigo, "I'm too tired even to watch, I will say good night. I'm off to slumberland."

"I'm too tired even to dance one round but I'll just watch for a short time." Amerigo replied yawning.

He moved on out to get a closer look at the dancers. Suddenly he found himself looking into two bright eyes. They were twinkling with merriment. The eyes belonged to a charming young girl. She in a playful manner said, "Sir, I beseech a dance with you."

Conquering his usual fainting courage when in the presence of the opposite sex, Amerigo clumsily put out his arms and they were off in a whirl. When there was a pause in the music, together they made their way to the side of the crowd. All of Amerigo's weariness had vanished as well as his timidity.

"You must be my fairy princess. Tell me your name," he begged.

"Later," she teased. "The music is calling." Off they danced to a lively tune.

The music again ceased and they made their way through the crowd. Eagerly Amerigo asked, "What is your name? And where do you live?" He felt as if he must know everything about this lovely maiden who had danced into his life.

"It is Elena," she said gaily. "And I'm no fairy princess. I'm just an ordinary girl."

"You__ ordinary! Never! You will always be a fairy princess to me," retorted Amerigo. "There will be more dancing tomorrow night. Will you come?"

"Would you like for me to come?" teased Elena.

"Yes, and you must come the next night and the next night. Now that I have found my fairy princess I won't let her go," said Amerigo with feeling.

"I'll come tomorrow night but now it is late, I must leave," replied Elena.

"One more dance," he pleaded, and again they were in each other's arms dancing.

When the music stopped, Elena reached up and kissed him lightly on the cheek and whispered, "Until tomorrow night." And then disappeared quickly into the crowd.

He ran after her calling, "Elena, Elena!" Although he searched everywhere in the piazza, she was gone. At last he gave up and made his way home; thinking, "Maybe she'll come back tomorrow. She promised."

Amerigo could scarcely wait until the next evening. He served the wine and kept the wine coolers but all the time he was wondering, "Will she come?" He did not lightly joke or exchange greetings with the guests or other pages as he usually did.

"You are mighty quiet tonight," observed Piero. "You must have made merry until the wee hours of the morn."

"Will you remain for the dance tonight?" inquired Amerigo ignoring the remark.

"No," retorted Piero. "Emilie's parents refused to let her stay for public dancing in the piazza and she has asked me to stop by her house."

"That will be nice," replied Amerigo. He was somewhat relieved for he did not want to share Elena with anyone, even Piero.

As soon as the feasting was over, Amerigo hurried to the spot where he and Elena first met.

"Would she come?" he wondered as he peered through the crowd. Suddenly, she was there and again they were in each other's arms dancing. The next night and the next night, they met at the same place and at the same time. They developed a closeness unusual for such a short time.

At the end of the third night, Amerigo asked anxiously, "The festival will be over tomorrow night. You must tell me where you live. I must know."

"Tomorrow night," she promised and again melted into the crowd. And Amerigo had to be satisfied.

The next night Elena was waiting for him and her manner was no longer gay. They danced without speaking for some time. Then she took his arm and together they made their way out of the crowd and found a secluded spot on the bank of the Arno.

Amerigo reached into his pocket and pulled out a golden locket, and gently fastened it around her neck. "Why are you so quiet tonight?" asked Amerigo. "Just because this is the last night of the festival doesn't mean that we can't keep on seeing each other."

"Yes, it does," Elena went on to explain. "I am a gypsy. Tomorrow we leave for the South. I won't see you again. Thank you for this locket. I'll keep it always and I'll wear it to remember you by but tonight we must say goodby."

"I can't let you go," he cried, as he pulled her toward him and kissed her forehead and then her lips.

Elena pulled away from him. "I must go," she told him
quietly. "I am a gypsy. I could never be a Florentine even if our
parents would agree to it. My father is a stern man. He has arranged
a marriage for me with an older gypsy. I will have to obey him. If
not he would kill us both."

"Oh," sobbed Amerigo. "I love you," and again he pulled her
close and covered her face and neck with kisses.

"I love you, too, Amerigo," whispered Elena. Her arms
tightened about him and as they lay in each other's arms, he opened her
blouse and rained kisses on her firm breast. Feelings he hardly knew
he possessed took control of him. Their warm bodies melted into each
other and Amerigo felt an erection and the embrace was complete. It
was a moment of ecstasy.

"You are mine," he cried. "I won't let you go." They lay
side by side in each other's arms. Amerigo refused to loosen his grip
until finally they fell asleep.

Elena woke first. She gently disengaged herself from his
embrace. She straightened her rumpled clothes and whispered softly so
as not to wake the sleeping youth. "I love you, Amerigo. Please
forgive me but I must obey my father. If I didn't he would kill us
both. It will be better if we never see each other again. Goodbye, my
love." She took one last look at the sleeping youth and quickly moved
away.

The sun was rising when Amerigo awoke. He was
bewildered. Where was Elena? Hastily he got up and looked about
him. The festival was over and all had gone home. Elena was
nowhere in the Piazza. He hurried to where the gypsy camp had been.
It was gone. They had silently moved to the south in the wee morning

hours. He finally realized that she was gone. He remembered her words. "My father is a stern man. He would kill us both." At that time, he felt that he had rather die than lose her but he did not want her to have to die too.

He was a sad young man as he returned to the Vespucci home. "Will I ever see her again?" he wondered. He felt as if his heart would break.

Later that day, he sought out his uncle and teacher, Giorgio Antonio, to get his advice.

"Amerigo," said his uncle gravely, "Life is never easy. Maybe Elena is wiser than you. No doubt, she realized that you are too young and that such a marriage could never be. Treasure her memory and remember that we Italians believe that 'Everything will sort itself out.'"

Chapter V

Amerigo Goes to Rome

It was the year 1472. Amerigo was eighteen years old, the age when many young people put their childhood behind them and begin to assume the responsibilities of adulthood. Two events happened during 1472 that helped him grow up. One was the death of his grandfather, Old Amerigo. This event made him ponder over the direction of his life. "I must try to be more like him," he thought, "I must study harder and remember his counsel." The other event was a trip to Rome with his uncle, Giorgio Antonio. This was Amerigo's first trip out of Florence and brought him in contact with people of different viewpoints. It gave him a broader view of the world.

Early in 1472, Old Amerigo had celebrated his seventy-second birthday. Failing health forced him to retire from his office as notary to the Signoria but he retained an active interest in the affairs of Florence. Whenever the weather permitted he was up and about. He became a familiar and dignified figure as he walked with his cane down the streets of his beloved city. He often stopped to chat with a fellow wool guild member or to listen to a discussion in the Signoria. It was said that Leonardo da Vinci used old Amerigo's face in his portrait of an old man.

Gradually he walked more slowly and his walks around Florence became less frequent. Soon he was too unsteady on his feet to go up and down the great stone steps and had to remain indoors. Finally he took to his bed. Even then he was not lonely or neglected, for the members of the large Vespucci family often visited him. He was much revered and loved and visits to see him were not sad occasions. He was cheerful and often joked with his sons and grandsons.

Soon it became evident that the old man was near death. Amerigo and his three brothers were asked to come to his bedside. Old Stagio told them their grandfather had not long to live so they were four solemn young men as they stood beside his bed.

The old man looked at them keenly and said, "You boys know, and I know, that soon I'll be crossing over to that great beyond. You must cease being so downcast, for to me it will be a great adventure. There comes a time when all mortals must step over that line, and for an old man of seventy-two it is a quiet release, a release from an old worn-out body.

Listen to what I have to say and cease being sad. I've lived more than the three score and ten years promised in the Scriptures. I have experienced both good and bad times and have learned much, both from men living today and from the ancients. I cannot transfer that knowledge and experience to you and perhaps would not if I could. Each must be free to live your own life. You will have to make your own mistakes, and I hope you learn from them. You must solve your own problems. Be doers. Remember that the Vespucci are and have been busy workers, like the wasps on our coat of arms. The worst kind of life a man can lead is a sterile one, a life that is selfishly devoted to one's own pleasures. Now, I have lived most of my life within the walls of Florence. You probably won't, for the world is changing and you must change with it.

The old man caught his breath and rested briefly. The four boys stood silently by, close to tears. The grandfather noticed this and continued, "Now, in a few days there will be a funeral procession marching down the streets of Florence. It will be my funeral procession and my body will lie on a platform draped in black and will be drawn by black horses. You will be marching beside me and all the members of my wool guild will be marching in front. They will all be dressed in black and some may even be weeping," chuckled the old man as if he was relishing the sight of his funeral. "Now you boys must not weep," continued Old Amerigo. "If you do, somehow or other I'll find a way to tell you to stop. Remember I'm still a raspy Old Vespucci wasp."

The boys walked out with smiles on their faces. The man's words had dried up their tears. He fell back on his pillow exhausted from such a long speech but on his face was a quiet look of satisfaction. He knew he had made his point.

Not too many days later the predicted funeral procession was making its way down the streets of Florence. Bells tolled, shops were closed, and doors were hung in black velvet. The members of Old Amerigo's wool guild all dressed in somber black and carrying banners headed the procession. They were followed by black robed priests, each carrying a lighted candle. On a black draped platform drawn by four black horses was Old Amerigo's body. The family also dressed in black and carrying lighted candles walked beside the platform. Behind them marched all the dignitaries of Florence. After them came many town's people for Old Amerigo had been a popular gonfaloniere and a well-known member of the Signoria.

It was a solemn and spectacular procession. No sound was heard except the sound of horses' hoofs. As Amerigo walked beside the casket a tear fell from his eyes. He thought of his grandfather's words and looked up. He saw a wasp lighting on the rear end of one of the black horses. The steed gave one loud neigh, paused, then settled down again to a steady walk. All the horses had pricked up their ears and their steady walk seemed little more lively. Amerigo dried his tears and half smiled. He glanced at his brothers. They too had seen the wasp. Their weeping had ceased and they managed a wan smile. In fact the mood of the whole procession seemed less solemn as it proceeded to Old Amerigo's resting place. It was what the old man had hoped.

Several days later the family gathered to settle the estate. Since Old Stagio was the oldest son, he was the sole heir. He inherited the handsome stone house and Peretola. Elisabetta and Old Stagio decided to remain in their old comfortable house and gave the big house to Antonio, their eldest son. Antonio was beginning a promising career as a lawyer and would soon be married. Later he would follow his father and grandfather and become the Priori of the Signoria.

Elisabetta was delighted with Catarina, the betrothed wife of Antonio. She and Antonio were to produce eight Vespucci children, and soon the old stone house was again teeming with footsteps and laughter. Old Amerigo would have been glad.

Now, Old Stagio was rather indifferent to money. He valued it only as a way of enjoyment for his family and friends. He continued to let the cousins live at Peretola and often pooled his money with Giorgio Antonio to buy old Greek manuscripts.

The trip to Rome that had been planned before Old Amerigo's death had been postponed. Now, Giorgio Antonio resumed his plans.

It was decided that Amerigo would go with him for the trip was not easy and often dangerous. "It will give Amerigo a look at Rome and life outside of Florence." said old Stagio.

A new pope, Sextus IV, had been installed the year before and Giorgio Antonio and other monks wanted to visit him. He would carry some gifts from Lorenzo who was anxious to keep on good terms with the new Pope. He realized the importance of the papacy in Italy and in the entire Christian world. It was a lesson instilled in him by his father and grandfather. Lorenzo's gifts were two marble busts, one of the Roman emperor Caesar Augustus and other of Agrippa, Caesar Augustus' famous general.

Amerigo and his Uncle Giorgio with other monks and pilgrims set out on their sixty mile journey. They rode donkeys and traveled on the old Roman road laid out by Julius Caesar so many years before. They stopped overnight at friendly monasteries. To pass the time much interesting conversation took place among the travelers. The monks were mostly learned men and some pilgrims were Greek scholars. Amerigo listened eagerly and asked questions. Much talk was about the new philosophy known as Humanism. Giorgio had been one of the first Florentine's to embrace this new philosophy. It encouraged the study of the ancient manuscripts and also encouraged man to seek a rational meaning to all things. Humanism stressed the dignity of man. It gave man the courage to question 'WHY'. Many barriers set up in the so called 'Dark Ages' no longer were absolute. They could be breached. It held that it was right for man to be creative. This philosophy made sense to Amerigo.

"When did Humanism begin?" he asked.

"It was after the year 1000, the first millennium. Many believed that Christ would return at the turn of the century," was the answer from a monks.

"Why did they believe this? Was it the Church's teaching?" asked a pilgrims.

"No church has ever sanctioned that belief, nevertheless it was the widely held belief," explained Giorgio. "Many people spent the night in a church praying, expecting the end of the world at midnight."

"If the Church did not teach about it, what caused the people to believe it?" asked another pilgrim.

"The belief was based on the twentieth chapter of Revelations," Uncle Giorgio answered. "And when the end did not occur the people were astounded."

"What did the people do then?" inquired Amerigo intensely interested.

"They gradually came to know that they had to go on living. They went back to the plow and spinning wheels," explained Giorgio.

"Another great event that started men to thinking and set the stage for the new philosophy was the Crusade of 1200, the only really successful Crusade. Jerusalem was conquered. Ancient knowledge of the Greeks that had been saved by the Arabs was recovered. The writings of Aristotle were soon to be translated," continued one of the Greek scholars.

"The reading and discussion of them set men to thinking. They decided that since God created man in his own image, he wanted man to be creative too," continued Giorgio. "Men came to question why? Why could no man venture beyond the Pillars of Hercules?

Marco Polo had travelled to the Great Sinus and had returned. Also they asked, 'Why was seeking wealth so wrong?' Men of wealth could do much good with their money. Soon universities were established and men sought to recover the learning of the past."

"And now in the 15th century we are beginning a new era," observed another monk. "Men are seeking a better and safer route to the Indies."

The conversations lasted long into the night. Amerigo listened and resolved that he, like Aristotle, would seek rational answers to all things.

After several days the travelers arrived in Rome. Amerigo was impressed at the grandeur of the Roman ruins. "Rome must have been a splendid city," thought Amerigo.

The visit to the pope was one Amerigo was to remember although Michelangelo's great dome was not in place. Neither were the famous paintings in the Sistine Chapel, but any audience with a pope is an impressive occasion.

Soon the uncle and nephew were on their way back to Florence. Riding side by side on their donkeys, they discussed their visit with the pope.

"Pope Sextus seemed glad to get the gifts," observed Amerigo, "but he did not greet you as warmly as he did the other monks."

"You are observant," promptly replied his uncle, "Pope Sextus is not pleased with Lorenzo. He has requested a loan from the Medici Bank and Lorenzo is putting him off."

" Putting off a pope could be dangerous," returned Amerigo. "Why is Lorenzo putting him off? Is the sum exorbitant?"

"Not exactly," explained Giorgio, "The sum is 40,000 ducats, a princely sum, but that is not the real reason. The pope wants the loan so he can buy the town of Imola for his nephew, Piero Riario. Lorenzo wants to buy Imola, himself, for he thinks it necessary for the defense of Florence, and he certainly doesn't want it to come under the influence of the papacy." And after a period of thoughtful silence, Giorgio continued, "It may be harder for Lorenzo to keep on good terms with the papacy than it was for his father and grandfather."

"Why?" questioned Amerigo.

"Sextus IV seems very ambitious. He is seeking much political power along with his great spiritual power. In the few months since he was consecrated he has made six nephews cardinals and granted favors to other relatives and some of them are rascals, I understand, and some of these rascals have received profitable lordships in the Papal States.

"How will this affect Florence?" Amerigo persisted. "We are the strongest city in Italy"

"Yes, but in the past popes have controlled all of Italy and Sextus seemed determined to again bring all of Italy under his influence. He is shrewd and cunning and may be ruthless in his quest for power. We will just have to hope things will work out for the best."

Soon the travelers were in sight of a large country house. "That is our destination," exclaimed Giorgio. "It is the home of Donati Accivinoli Fillipo. I visited him some years ago. We worked together in the study of mathematics and geography. He is a friend and co-worker with Paolo del Puzzo Toscanelli.

"Toscanelli, the famous scientist!" exclaimed Amerigo, "Will he be here?"

"Probably not but the famous map that he and Fillipo are making is here," responded Giorgio. "Fillipo asked us here to see it."

The visitors had been spotted long before they reached the house, and Fillipo was coming out to greet them. "You do us honor, Giorgio, by visiting our humble home."

"We are looking forward to seeing your map and it will be good to talk with you again. Much has changed since we worked together," said Giorgio. "Fillipo, this is my nephew. He, too, is interested in geography and mathematics. He has traveled with me on my trip to Rome.

"The map that you and Toscanelli are making is of special interest in Florence," said Amerigo in greeting. "Is Toscanelli here?"

"No," responded Fillipo, "but I am sure he will be sorry to have missed you. He is lecturing at the University in Pisa, but the map is here. We will be glad to get your opinion of it."

"We will find it interesting, I'm sure," answered Giorgio, "but we will be just as interested in your ideas about our changing earth. The Fortunate Islands have been rediscovered and more and more of the coast of Africa are being explored.

"It will be my pleasure to exchange ideas with you and to compare Ptolemy's map with ours, but first you must have some food and drink. You must be famished," said Fillipo, as he led the way into the villa. After being refreshed they talked until a late hour.

The next morning the two large maps were unrolled. The updated map was of much interest for all the commercial houses of Florence, for at that time, all of Italy was hoping for a safer route to the Indies. The desert route was increasingly dangerous and Egypt charged an exorbitant tariff for goods being transported across her land. The once lucrative trade with the East had slowed to only a trickle.

The Toscanelli map suggested a sea route to the Indies around the southern tip of Africa. "Now," Fillipo disclosed, "Toscanelli is suggesting the possibility of a western sea route to the Indies straight across the great Ocean Sea."

The three men studied the two maps carefully. The Toscanelli map was on a large rolled parchment, beautifully decorated with water colors, but was much the same as Ptolemy's. Nicolo Nicolli had copied Ptolemy's map many years ago, and left it in the care of Toscanelli. He was one of the early humanist.

Both maps showed the Red Sea, Arabia, the Arabian Desert, the Persian Gulf, the Indus River, the Ganges River, and the Great Sinus. The Great Sinus or Cathy was the European name for China. On Ptolemy's map but not on Toscanelli's was a cape that he called Catigara. He located it eight and one half degrees south of the equator.

"Toscanelli still agrees with most of Ptolemy's ideas but he is not sure about Catigara and he doubts Ptolemy's distance to the Great Sinus. He still seeks out travelers from the East and listens carefully to what they say. He is always seeking to separate truth from superstition," explains Fillipo.

"If Ptolemy is right," noted Amerigo, "to get to the Great Sinus, one must first sail south then west."

"Yes, and although both Toscanelli and Ptolemy agree that the earth is a globe, Ptolemy doubted that men could live on the underside of it. Toscanelli believes it possible," continued Fillipo. "In 1464, he wrote a letter to the canon of the Lisbon Cathedral suggesting that he thought it possible to reach the Indies by sailing both to the east or by sailing to the west. He long ago had suggested to Prince Henry, the Navigator, the idea of reaching the Indies by sailing south around Africa."

"Did the Portuguese try out the theory?" asked Amerigo.

"No," answered Fillipo, "Prince Henry died and new ideas died with him. The king was busy developing the profitable trade on the west African coast around Cape Verde. Gold had been discovered there and also the slave trade was profitable.

"But I thought they were interested in seeking a sea route to the Indies," commented Amerigo.

"They are now," continued Fillipo, but they are still seeking a sea route around Africa. By doing that they can hug the African shore. No one has dared sailing westward yet to get to the East, but recently an Italian seaman residing in Portugal has written to Toscanelli asking his opinion about sailing westward to the Indies. He had heard about his letter to the canon. Toscanelli has sent him a copy."

"Trade with the Indies is certainly crippled now just when the demand for their spices and other exotic goods is rising. The time is right to seek the water route," observed Giorgio thoughtfully.

"It would seem so," Fillipo replied. "Ptolemy's idea for lines of latitude and longitude would help make such a voyage possible. He determined nearly perfect latitude but did not live long enough to determine longitude. Knowing both would help on such a voyage. He challenged future scientists to solve that problem of longitude."

Amerigo was to remember that challenge as he and Giorgio set out for Florence the next morning and again twenty years later when in Seville.

They were greeted warmly when they returned home. A big dinner was held in their honor. It was a fitting end to this special trip. It was very special for Amerigo and gave him a broader view of the world and set him thinking of Ptolemy's challenge.

Chapter VI

The Festival To Honor Giuliano Medici

It was the year 1475. The streets of Florence were again decked out with banners and flowers and again the town's people were gathering for another splendid parade and tournament. This celebration was to honor Giuliano Medici, Lorenzo's younger brother. He was twenty-one years old.

Amerigo and his friend, Piero Soderini, were also again standing by waiting to take their places in the parade. This time they would be knights and take part in the tournament as well as in the parade.

"I am thankful for my fencing lessons at San Marco," observed Amerigo to Piero. "For now I'm skilled enough to take part in the tournament."

"And I, also," replied Piero. "It is better to be participating in it than just watching it."

"Here comes Giuliano and Simonetta," exclaimed Amerigo, "Isn't she beautiful. No wonder Giuliano in love with her and chose her for the Queen of Beauty."

"Look at her gown! Botticelli designed it as well as Giuliano's armor," cried Piero.

"Simonetta looks every inch a queen," admired Amerigo. "I expect Botticelli is in love with her , too. He painted her as Venus in his 'The Birth of Venus.'"

"No doubt about it and I heard him say he would use her as his model for all of his lovely ladies. And if he's not in love with her, he's about the only man in Florence that is not," continued Amerigo.

"What about you, Amerigo? You do not seek the company of ladies very much. Could it be that you are pining away for Simonetta?" teased Piero.

"Of course not," was Amerigo's prompt retort, but he blushed. Piero noticed his discomfort but did not comment.

"Amerigo must have a secret love," he mused, "But I won't pry. He will tell me when he gets ready."

For the next few minutes Amerigo was quiet. He had never told Piero or anyone but Uncle Giorgio about Elena. It still hurt even to think of her. "Where is she ?" he wondered. "Is she happy with her gypsy husband? If I were a painter, it would be her face that I would put on canvas."

Now, the parade was about to begin. Giuliano handed Simonetta into the carriage. The people cheered. This parade seemed to be generating even more excitement and anticipation than Lorenzo's parade, for while Lorenzo was loved and respected, Giuliano was adored. He was a handsome youth and was warm and friendly to all. He was the idol of all the young maidens. His strength and skill in fencing, jousting, and horseback riding made him a model for all young men. The older women nodded with approval as he rode by on the streets of Florence. His smile seemed just for them. Even the older men were impressed when he stopped, as he often did, to exchange a word or two with them. No doubt about it, he was the "golden boy" of Florence.

And the occasion was even more memorable because he had chosen Simonetta Vespucci as his Queen of Beauty. She, too, was popular with both the old and young for not only was she beautiful to look at, but she was also kind and gentle.

She had come to Florence several years before from Genoa as the bride of Marco Vespucci, a cousin of Amerigo. Because of her unusual beauty and her charm she was chosen as a model not only by Botticelli but also for Ghirlandaio, and other contemporary painters. She was described as having golden hair, blue eyes, ivory skin, and the face of an angel.

Poets wrote verses to her. Poliziano, possibly the greatest of Italian poets of that time, wrote this poem in her honor at the time of the festival.

> White is the maid and
>> white the robe around her,
> With buds and rose and
>> thin grass pied,
> Enwreathed folds of golden
>> tresses crowned her

Shadowing her forehead fair
with modest pride.
The wild wood smiled: the
thicket where he found her,
To ease his anguish, bloomed
on every side.
Serene she sits with gesture
queenly mild,
And with her brow tempers
the tempest wild.

Lorenzo who also wrote beautiful poetry wrote these few lines about her at the same time:

Bright shining star! Thy
radiance in the sky
Dos't rob the neighboring
stars of all their light.
Why art thou with unwonted
splendor bright,
Why with great Phoebus
dos't thy dare to vie!

Simonetta was as lovely as the poems she inspired. She was beautifully dressed in a satin gown encrusted in precious stones. Giuliano was also handsomely dressed. It is said that, "Something in the Renaissance heart seemed to crave splendor and display" as well as beauty. This celebration was one that must have satisfied all, for it was truly magnificent. It was perhaps the most splendid of Lorenzo's famous festivals and certainly earned him the title of "The Magnificent". Simonetta was crowned the Queen of Beauty by

Giuliano. He then was awarded the prize trophy for his skill in the tournament, as it had been pre-agreed. It was a joyful occasion but would be the last for a time.

Chapter VII

The Pazzi Conspiracy

It was the year 1478. The streets of Florence were no longer gay. No banners were flying and the Florentines went about their daily business in a quiet and somber mood. It had been that way since the death of the lovely Simonetta Vespucci. She was only twenty-two when she died, a victim of the then deadly disease, consumption. Somehow the joy of living that had so characterized the Florentines seemed not able to bounce back.

The widening breach between Lorenzo and the pope was also a concern among all the people. When Lorenzo was slow in granting Pope Sextus IV, the money with which to buy the township of Imola, the pope turned to a rival bank, the bank of the Pazzi family. The Pazzi family was an older Florentine family than the Medici and were jealous of them. They very much wanted to wrest the control of Florence from them so they eagerly provided the loan to gain the help of the pope.

Lorenzo felt so threatened by the actions of the pope that he proposed an alliance with Venice and Milan to "keep the peace". This move angered the pope even more. The pope then arranged a marriage between one of his nephews and an illegitimate daughter of the King of Naples. The King of Naples had always been a friend of Lorenzo, but now Lorenzo realized that he could no longer count Naples as an ally. To complicate the uneasy situation the ruler of Milan, Goliazza Maria Sforgo, had been assassinated. His son and heir was only seven years old. His wife declared herself regent. Although she was firm in her resolve to back Florence, Lorenzo knew that several uncles disputed her claim, so he was afraid that he could not depend on help from Milan. Danger seemed to be closing in on Florence from every side. All were waiting for the pope to strike.

It happened on a beautiful Easter morning in a most unlikely place, the Cathedral in Florence. The Vespucci family was all on their way to the celebration of the eleven o'clock mass. The cathedral like the Baptistery was only a ten minute walk from the Vespucci home. Old Stagio and Mono Lisa led the way. They were followed by Giorgio Antonio and Guido Antonio. The four boys walked behind.

Suddenly Mona Lisa stopped and exclaimed, "The front door! I forgot to pull the latch. Run back, Amerigo, and see that it is fastened. You are the fastest runner and I'm sure you can get to the cathedral in time for mass."

Amerigo turned quickly and was off. He was well aware that thieves often picked Easter Sunday Mass as a time to rob the citizenry. Barring doors at that time was very important. In a short time, the latch was in place and Amerigo was on his way back to the Cathedral. He heard running feet and a voice called frantically, "Wait, wait! The Cathedral! Show me the way to the Cathedral! I've rushed all the way from Pisa. I overheard of a plot to kill Lorenzo. My horse gave out and now I must warn him in time. The plan is to assassinate him in the Cathedral."

Amerigo was quick to grasp the danger, "Follow me," he yelled and quickened his pace. The young runners reached the great doors of the Cathedral just as the host was being raised at the sound of the Sanctuary bell.

"Lorenzo! Lorenzo! Watch out," they shouted. Lorenzo turned just in time. The assassins's daggers missed their mark and only grazed his shoulder. Lorenzo flung off his cape, drew his sword, and turned on his assassins. They fled in terror.

For the moment there was a stunned silence in the great room, then began a great commotion. Lorenzo's friends yelled, "Don't let them get away," as they hustled Lorenzo off to the safety of the sacristy.

"Giuliano! Giuliano!" cried the wounded Lorenzo. "Warn him! They will try to kill him too."

Several hastened to find Giuliano but it was too late. His assassins had not missed their mark and he lay mortally wounded on the cathedral floor.

Amerigo pushed his way through the frightened crowd and joined his family. "What happened, Amerigo? Are you all right?" they asked excitedly.

"Yes," Amerigo gasped, for now he was the breathless one, "I brought the man who warned Lorenzo. He had overheard the plot in Pisa and had rushed all the way to warn Lorenzo. It is a plot by the pope and the Pazzi family to seize the rule of Florence. As I pushed through the mob," he continued, "I heard that Lorenzo had escaped with only a slight wound but that Giuliano had been killed."

"Stay here," Guido Antonio commanded the stunned family. "You will be safer away from the mob. I will go see what I can find out."

Mona Lisa was weeping, "How terrible! How terrible! Giuliano dead!"

"Maybe it is not true, Elisabetta," said Stagio, as he put a comforting arm around his weeping wife. "We can pray that it is not true. Guido will find out."

Soon Guido was back, "I'm afraid Amerigo heard right. Giuliano is dead and Lorenzo wounded. Come Giorgio. You, too, Stagio. We must hasten to the piazza. All hands will be needed there."

"Yes," agreed Old Stagio, now taking command. "I agree all will be needed. You, Amerigo and Bernardo, take your Mother home and bolt the door. Stay in until we come. Antonio, you and Girolamo, come with us. Florence is in trouble."

The older men hastened off. Amerigo took his mother's arm and with Bernardo on her other side gradually they made their way to the cathedral door.

"Look the other way, Mona Lisa," Amerigo begged, for he wanted to spare her the sight of Giuliano's body lying in a pool of blood on the cathedral floor. She, as well as the rest of the family had been very fond of Giuliano.

The three made the short walk home in record time and soon

were inside the stone house with the doors barred. They waited not daring to voice their thoughts, "Would there be fighting? Would there be more bloodshed?"

Bernardo said finally, "If they hurt Old Stagio or Antonio or Girolamo, what will we do? I wish father had let me go."

Amerigo kept quiet but he knew how Bernardo felt for he, too, wished he were in the piazza.

Uncle Giorgio was the first to return, "Florence is safe," he quickly told the eager group. "Most of the assassins have been captured and their armed men have fled. Lorenzo is not badly wounded. He was even able to come to the piazza and take command."

"Tell us everything," begged Bernardo.

"It was Caesare Petruca, our Gonfaloniere, who saved the day." Giorgio continued. "It seems that after stabbing Giuliano his two assassins escaped and hastened to the piazza and handed Caesare a bull from Pope Sextus commanding him to surrender. Old Caesare did not accept the bull but drew his sword and pushed them into a closet, locked the door, and rang the bell summoning the people.

"My! Caesare was brave!" marvelled young Bernardo. "I wish I could have been there. What is a bull?" asked the puzzled Bernardo.

"It is an official order from the pope," answered Giorgio.

"But the pope didn't order the assassination of Lorenzo and Giuliano, he couldn't have!" exclaimed Elisabetta.

"No, not exactly," answered Giorgio, "but he agreed to a coup to throw them out of office."

"But tell us more," begged Amerigo. "What happened then?"

"Montesecco and his band of condottiere rode onto the piazza crying 'Liberty! Liberty!' They expected the people to rally around them, but they miscalculated the popularity of Lorenzo. The people turned fiercely on Montesecco and his men. By this time hundreds were pouring onto the piazza. Montesecco and his band quickly retreated.

"And then, what happened?" the eager boys asked when Giorgio seemed through.

"Old Caesare turned the two assassins over to the people and told them that they were Giuliano's murderers. The people promptly hanged them and now their bodies are dangling from the scaffold in the piazza," further disclosed Giorgio.

"How horrible! How terrible!" Mona Lisa moaned, "but tell us of Stagio, and my boys. Are they all right?"

"Yes," Giorgio reassured her. "Soon, no doubt, they will all return home."

And sure enough the four men soon were at the door. "How are things now?" asked Giorgio.

"All is going well, for Lorenzo's presence quieted the mob," explained Old Stagio. "Giuliano's murderers were Francisco Pazzi and his friend. Their bodies are still dangling from the scaffold. The two that attempted to murder Lorenzo were captured in the cathedral and quickly put to death. They were priests. Now order seems to be restored and a group is in hot pursuit of Montesecco."

"Will Montesecco attack in the night?" wondered Amerigo.

"Possibly not," responded their father. "He knows he is outnumbered and realizes that the people will not rebel against Lorenzo."

There was very little rest in the Vespucci home that night, but the next day it was learned that Montesecco had been captured. When it was learned that he had refused to take part in the murders in the cathedral, he was allowed a soldier's death instead of hanging.

Lorenzo's troubles were not over for the pope promptly excommunicated him and put all Florence on probation. The pope was also able to get most of the Italian cities to join him. His power was much respected and all seemed dismal for Florence.

Chapter VIII

Amerigo Goes To Paris

It was still the year 1478. Most of the Pazzi family clan had been executed or banished. Other Pazzis had fled the wrath of Lorenzo and the Florentine people. The murder of the popular Giuliano had rallied all the populace to Lorenzo's side.

Lorenzo lost no time in confiscating all of the Pazzi property in Florence and in the nearby area. Antonio Vespucci, Amerigo's brother, was appointed trustee of those vast holdings. Guido Antonio Vespucci was dispatched to Paris to confiscate the Pazzi holdings there and to close down the Pazzi banks. He asked Amerigo to go with him as his attache or private secretary.

It was Amerigo's first time out of Italy. He could learn first hand what the rest of the continent was like. In his copy book Amerigo had written that he hoped "to go, to see, and to know" and now a new world was opening up to him.

Amerigo was now twenty four years of age. He had a sturdy

well built body but was only slightly above medium height. He would need a strong body to survive the trip to Paris, because it was necessary to cross the lofty Alps.

The plan called for stops in Bologna, Milan, and Lyon on the way. Guido Antonio was then the most prominent statesman in Florence. He was well known as a prominent lawyer, a man of letters, as well as an able diplomat. His mission, besides taking care of the Pazzi affairs, was to seek the backing of Louis XI, the King of France, in Florence's controversy with Pope Sextus. He was also to seek the goodwill of the Duke of Bologna and the help of the cities of Milan and Lyon. It was a very important mission. Much of Florence's safety depended on his success.

Guido was well prepared for this mission for he was a polished diplomat, subtle and refined. It is probable that many of Machiavelli's methods were learned from Guido. He believed that power rested in popular prestige and was against the personal dictatorships of a prince. He realized, however, that all stable governments must have a strong man at the top and he approved of Lorenzo's rule.

There were two hundred in the cavalcade that set out for Paris. It was early in the fall for they wanted to get through the lofty Alps before the heavy winter storms. Going with Amerigo and Guido were clerks, secretaries, each with their personal servants. There were cooks, hostlers, baggage handlers also soldiers to protect the group, a blacksmith to shoe the horses, and an armorer to keep the armor and weapons in repair. Other travelers also asked to be a part of the cavalcade, for it was always safer to travel in groups.

The first stop for negotiation would be in Bologna fifty miles to the North, but the first night was spent in a monastery several miles south of that town. There Guido discussed the government of Bologna with the old abbot who was well-known for his wisdom. You may be sure that Amerigo was quite attentive.

Guido opened the discussion with this question, "How do you believe Bologna feels about the dispute between Lorenzo and the Pope. Which one do you think he will it favor?"

"The history of Bologna, like that of all Italian cities has been a struggle for power between the ruling classes and the papacy. Most have suffered conspiracies similar to your Pazzi conspiracy."

"I know Giovanni Bentivolio holds power in Bologna today. Does he have the backing of the populi?" inquired Guido.

"He seems as popular in Bologna as Lorenzo is in Florence," responded the monk.

"There is a difference in the way they rule, I understand," stated Guido. "In Bologna, Giovanni arms the people. On the other hand Lorenzo rules by disarming them. Which is the better way, I wonder! Perhaps time will tell. Lorenzo now needs Bologna's backing. My mission to Bologna is to make sure that Giovanni supports Lorenzo in this dispute."

"Yes, I have heard," returned the monk. "We don't travel much, but we hear much from travelers such as yourselves."

"How do you think we will be received?" questioned Guido.

"I doubt that Bologna would support Sextus, for it doesn't want to be again dominated by the papacy and since the Bentivolios have suffered a similar tragedy to yours, I expect Giovanni will stand with Florence. Do you know about the Canetoli Conspiracy?" queried the monk.

"I have heard much about it but would like to know more and I'm sure, it will be of interest to Amerigo, my young secretary. Please tell us about it," asked Guido.

"It is a grim story," began the old monk. "When Giovanni Bentivolio was a very young child, his father was the duke. The Canetolis invited all the Bentivolios to a feast. Each Bentivolio man was seated beside a Canetoli. It was a long and splendid feast. Much wine was offered," continued the old man, "and the final course was daggers. At a signal, each Canetoli thrust his dagger into his neighbor's heart. The Bentivolios were wiped out."

"And now," Guido interrupted, "a Bentivolio is back in power. Some must have escaped."

"Yes," continued the old monk. "The children, for the Canetolis figured without knowing the popularity of the Bentivolios. Before they were able to take care of the children, another noble family, the Maressolli, with the help of the populi sought out all the Canetolis. They killed them, cut out their hearts and nailed them to the doors of the Bentivolios' palaces."

"It is a horrible story," agreed Amerigo. "And now in Florence, Lorenzo is seeking out all the Pazzis and is either putting them to death or banishing them for life. Is such revenge necessary?"

"It seems necessary," defended Guido. "I hope that there will come a time when all Italy is united under a stable government. Louis XI, I understand, seems to be uniting all France and also it seems that Queen Isabella and Ferdinand are uniting Spain. Italy will sooner or later, have to unify.

"But which Italian city would you choose as the ruler? Florence?" chuckled the old wise monk. "Venice would not agree to that, nor Rome, or even Bologna."

"That is our problem," returned Guido smiling. "Pride and the love of power is our enemy, not each other but we don't or won't admit it."

The next morning the cavalcade took leave of the old monk after thanking him and giving a generous offering for lodging and food, and continued the short way to Bologna.

Soon the two leaning towers of Bologna came into view. They were an impressive sight. Bologna, like Florence, was an Etruscan town that had come under the rule of Rome. It was at the foot of the Apennines and the meeting place of many roads, all built by the ancient Romans. The road north from Rome through Florence was the one on which Guido and his party were traveling. It was known as the Aemilian Way and extended northwest to Milan.

"I hope I can find time to visit the university here," observed Amerigo. "If I had attended a university, the one at Bologna would have been the university I would have chosen."

"It is one of the best," agreed Guido. "You would have chosen well. But here we are at the Palazza Comunale, Bologna's town hall. It is here that we are to meet the duke."

Looking up Amerigo saw the handsome figure of Duke Giovanni Bentivolio coming out to greet them.

"Welcome," he smiled as he greeted the party. "You are Guido Antonio Vespucci from Florence. Your messenger advised me of your arrival. You are indeed welcome."

The group was ushered into a large hall for refreshment but soon Guido and the duke were seriously discussing Florence's problem caused by the threat of the Pope.

"Bologna, for so long, was under Papal authority," the duke recalled. "And it never prospered under the heavy hand of the pope. Now it seems that Sextus IV is seeking to again put all Italy under the pope's authority. Yes, Florence is his first target but soon it will be Bologna, then Milan, then the rest.

"Then we must agree that this must not happen," was Guido's quick response.

"Yes," agreed the Duke. "We will stand with Florence."

This was especially gratifying news to Guido for he felt that the Duke probably was expressing the feeling of most Italian cities.

The stay in Bologna was pleasant and restful. Here the ambassador of the Duke of Ferrari joined the cavalcade as it continued on its way to Milan. It crossed the great ridge of the Apennines, past peasant cabins, churches, and past cattle grazing on the mountain side. Others beside Duke Ferrari and his party also joined the travelers. It was a slow journey on horseback across the rugged terrain but Amerigo enjoyed the company of the other secretaries and the travelers, some of which had come from far away places. As is often the case on such journeys, the travelers from all stations in life become friends and come to understand one another better. And so Amerigo's world widened. He learned to respect men in all stations in life.

Soon they reached the city of Milan, the gateway to the Alps.

Milan was rich and prosperous and Amerigo was delighted to be able to visit the city. He had been much impressed when the Duke of Milan, Goliazzo Maria Sforzo, had visited Florence. Sforzo had long been a firm ally of Lorenzo for he had been assisted to power by Cosimo, Lorenzo's grandfather.

Now Sforzo was dead, and Guido knew that in such a state of unrest he could depend on little help from Milan, he just paid his respect to Madam Sforzo. Guido did, however, meet with other diplomats who had come to Milan to confer with him. Amerigo was an interested observer. He continued learning the inner working of diplomats. He learned the value of working together and the necessity of compromise.

After this interesting conference Amerigo did get to view the great Gothic Cathedral in Milan. It was made of white marble and had a "forest of spires" and many marble statutes. The next morning the travelers continued on their way across the Alps on the way to Lyon.

They passed vineyards on the mountain sides and deep lakes between the lofty mountains. This scenery was spectacular and delighted the travelers. Not many had been this far from Florence before. Despite the exciting views the journey was hard and tedious. Often a horse faltered as a rock was unloosed by his foot. Gallantly, however, the horses walked on spurred on by kind words from their masters. The donkeys plodded along patiently. The cavalcade was able to follow the Rhone River valley route for some distance before they reached Lyon. The sight of the city was a welcome one. The weary travelers were glad to leave the Alps behind them before real winter set in.

Lyon was an old and charming city. It had been settled by the

Romans long ago. Now it was becoming known for its budding silk industry. At that time the city was a part of the French Crown, but it boasted a strong city council. Guido and his secretaries met with them and found them sympathetic to the problems of Florence. Lyon was important to Florence for economic reasons as well as political for it was an important Medici bank center.

After the business was attended to in Lyon, the cavalcade began the last leg of their long journey.

"My wearied body will be glad to get to Paris," exclaimed Amerigo. "How much farther do we have to go?"

"There are still quite a few miles, but it is downhill all the way, or at least we will think so after that tortuous climb over the Alps," disclosed Guido.

"About how long do you expect us to be in Paris?" inquired Amerigo.

"As long as it takes to complete our mission. I think it would be at least a year," answered Guido. "No doubt you will have time to get well acquainted with our French neighbors and I believe you will like them."

Chapter IX

The Year in Paris

It was the year 1480. Guido Antonio and Amerigo had been in Paris for more than a year. They would soon be returning across the Alps. From time to time messengers had brought news from Florence. The latest news was most heartening for normalcy was returning to that troubled city. Lorenzo, it seems, had seized upon a bold plan of going unattended directly to the King's Court at Naples. This plan was highly dangerous but by such daring, he won the admiration of the King of Naples and again persuaded him to become his ally. The populi of Florence were very proud of Lorenzo's bravery and rallied around him even more. Furthermore, messengers had carried Guido's good news back to Florence that Bologna and other cities to the north as well as France would stand with Lorenzo.

Guido Antonio had, with the help of Amerigo, almost finished their mission in Paris. They had confiscated the holdings of the Pazzi Family, closed down their banks, and now with the assurance of the good will of Louis XI, their mission was complete. They planned to return home in a fortnight.

"This year has flown by," thought Amerigo. "I wish Piero could have shared the excitement with me. I must write him about it. The following is the letter to Piero Soderini recounting his experience in Paris.

Paris, 1____

Dear Piero,

I want to tell you about my year in Paris. It has been quite an experience and I wish you could have come with us, but I'm sure your year has been eventful, too. I want to congratulate you on your coming marriage to Emilie. She was your choice and you hers. Your parents are wise. I'm sure you will be very happy.

And now to tell you about Paris. I shall never forget my excitement when the first view of the towers of the magnificent Notre Dame Cathedral came into view. Our journey had been long and tedious but now all weariness left me and I was all anticipation. Our first stop was a brief visit inside the Cathedral to thank God for our safe journey. When I looked up at the great rose window in the Cathedral, I was thrilled by its beauty. From that moment on I was held captive by the charm of this "City of Light."

Now Paris doesn't have great lighted boulevards or even as many paved streets as Florence does, but there is an excitement here. The city continues to hold me in thrall. Maybe it is the exquisite beauty of the Cathedral, the glamour of the King's Court with its lovely ladies, and the anticipation of seeing a real live king. Now, I still am thankful that Florence rejected the rule of nobles or a king. I'm proud of our democratic government, but there is a certain aura that surrounds a king and his court that thrills one.

I have spent many hours on affairs of state. Uncle Guido would have it no other way; nor would I have wished to shirk my duty, but much time was left for pleasure. Paris gives one many opportunities for enjoying oneself and I made good use of the time I had. Much of it has been in spent with the Court of Louis XI. Now as you probably know, most of the time the king holds court in Paris but often the whole court moves elsewhere in France. Although Paris has been the capital since the 400's, the capital and court have always moved around with the king. We spent much time in other parts of France. The French countryside is picturesque. Even the peasants seem to have an eye for beauty.

Many cities and most of the countryside are now under the rule of Louis XI. Uncle Guido is much impressed with the unity of France. He hopes one day that all Italy will come together into one strong nation. He admires Louis XI for continuing the process of unification that was begun many years ago by Charles VII and even before him.

Uncle Guido is also much impressed with Louis's prime minister, Philippe de Comines. Besides being a great statesman, he is an able writer of history. Guido believes it is Philippe's wise counsel that has guided the king. It is Philippe, too, that is especially interested in Florence's problems. He feels that the influence of Pope Sextus should be in the spiritual realm and not spill over into the political arena.

But I'm sure you will be more interested in the court life of Paris. The tales are true. It is gay. It is exciting. You have chided me in the past for not seeking the company of women. Here you don't have to seek them, they pursue you, and I, despite my lack of a title, have had a wonderful time. While much importance in Paris is attached to being of noble birth, I was acceptable because of being the attache to the Florentine Ambassador. Also, as we in Florence had heard much talk about Paris, they had heard much talk about us. Florence, it seems, enjoys in Paris a special reputation for its culture and just being a Florentine makes one interesting to the Pariesienne ladies.

Dancing is especially important in the French Court. Jewish dancing masters are much in demand. I must confess that I engaged one and have improved my skill and much of my time in France has been spent dancing. The basic dance is the Galliard. It is slow and stately and the one I was able to master. Some French dances feature leaping contortions. While I have enjoyed seeing others performing that type of dancing, you may be sure that I am not comfortable with such cavorting.

The ladies of the court sing, dance, and put on delightful plays. Pantomime is one of my favorites and Roslette is my favorite little French mademoiselle. She dances divinely and plays the oboe and tambourine. She is quite a flirt but a charming one. I first noticed her when she was walking for she has a special way of holding up her skirt to show off a dainty little foot. She has a special way, too, of holding up her fan to her eyes that disarms young men, especially one as unaccustomed to the wiles of women as I was. She also plays an excellent game of chess and backgammon. She would often beat me and I considered myself a skillful player. We have had many good times together and we will miss each other. She, you can be sure, is not desirous of leaving Paris and no doubt is waiting for a titled husband. I, on my part, found her a desirable and enjoyable companion, but marriage is not yet for me. We have parted as good friends.

Uncle Guido and I, with our companions, will leave Paris in a fortnight and begin our long rough journey across the Alps. We will make several stops along the way but will plan to be home in April or May if late snowstorms do not impede our way.

Before we depart from Paris we plan to go to the Saint Chapelle for morning prayer. It is such a holy place and where I have attended or participated in the mass for most of the past year. It was built in the 13th century to house the Crown of Thorns. It seems that this holy relic was purchased in Venice by Louis IX in 1239. We trust that the Christ who bravely wore this crown of thorns will safely lead us through the perilous Alps.

Farewell till spring,

Your friend,

Amerigo Vespucci

In Paris, Amerigo moved in a select circle and his association with the courtiers and ladies of the court trained him in the art of good living. He was blessed from childhood with a gift for friendship and from Guido Antonio, the diplomat, he learned to be discrete and never brusque. Amerigo's experiences while in Paris put the finishing touch on his education. It well prepared him for the life that lay ahead.

The trip home was, as expected, long and wearisome, but the cavalcade reached Florence about the time planned. Guido Antonio was pleased to report the results of the trip to Lorenzo, who also was pleased. Lorenzo quickly asked Guido to go to Rome to negotiate with the Pope Sextus. Since the King of Naples, after Lorenzo's visit, had abruptly withdrawn his aid from the Papacy, old Sextus, was changing his attitude toward Florence. Lorenzo was confident that with a little urging from Guido, he would lift the sanctions from Florence and his excommunication. Both had so hastily been declared after the Pazzi Conspiracy and both weighed heavily on the town. Guido immediately asked Amerigo to go to Rome with him, "You have served me well, Amerigo," said Guido. "Will you go as my attache to the Vatican. This, too, will be an important mission."

"No," Amerigo's father, Old Stagio answered for him. "I need Amerigo to carry on the family business. My health is deteriorating and Amerigo is my only son trained for business," and turning to Amerigo, he continued, "Please stay in Florence."

Amerigo was concerned because his father looked so frail and he immediately agreed to stay. He declined Guido's offer and for the next ten years was successfully engaged in the mercantile business in Florence.

Chapter X

Amerigo Goes to Work For the Medici

It was the year 1482. Old Stagio died that year. He had gradually weakened since Amerigo's return from Paris. Still, every morning he was up early and walked the short distance to his office. Amerigo admired his father's determination. He tried to assume more responsibility and was so glad that he had refused to go to Rome and had stayed in Florence to help his father. One morning Amerigo was awakened by a cry from Mona Lisa. "Come, Amerigo, I can't arouse your father."

Old Stagio had died in his sleep and another Vespucci funeral made its way through the streets of Florence. Many of his fellow Florentines joined in the funeral procession for he was a friend of all.

Toscanelli also died in 1482. Both events saddened Amerigo and much of Florence. Toscanelli was the famous Florentine scientist whose ideas and theories fascinated both Amerigo and his Uncle Giorgio.

For the two years since Guido and Amerigo had returned from Paris, Amerigo had been engaged in the banking and mercantile business of his father. His training and experience as a diplomat helped him become successful in this field. This expertise did not go unnoticed by the Medici.

Soon after his fathers death, Lorenzo di Pier Francisco de Medici came to Amerigo and said "I need a person experienced in trade and one who is free to travel to help take care of my affairs. When you have wound up your father's business, will you come to work for me?" he asked.

"It is true that I have almost finished with my father's business, but your offer will be a big step. Let me think about it," replied Amerigo.

With the help of his brother, Antonio, Amerigo was winding up his father's estate. Mona Lisa had moved into the big stone house with Antonio and Catarina. The place at Peretola had been sold. Girolamo who was now a monk took his inheritance and began a pilgrimage to the Holy Land. Bernardo was not ready to settle down either. He took his small share and embarked on an adventurous life. He left Florence. Soon Amerigo heard from him in Buda, Hungary. Amerigo was now free of family responsibilities.

The offer from Lorenzo di Pier was indeed tempting. The Medici had banks in Rome, Milan, Genoa, Venice, also in Lyon, Antwerp, Bruges, Avignon, Lubeck, Geneva, London, and in Spain, Valencia and Barcelona and interest in Seville. This offer would give Amerigo the opportunity "to go, to see, and to know." He still felt the same desire. It also would give him access to the Medici Library.

"What should he do?" he wondered. Although this Lorenzo

was a cousin of "the Magnificent," they represented rival political parties. Both were grandsons of the great Cosimo de Medici. Both had inherited equal fortunes. While Lorenzo the Magnificent had been involved in the affairs of state the other Lorenzo had concentrated on business so his holdings had greatly increased.

Both Lorenzos had been friends in their youth but now they were not on friendly terms. It seems that "the Magnificent" had had to borrow money from the other and as is often the case bitterness and resentment about money divided the two. Lorenzo di Pier who had grown up in the aristocratic party gave up his place and joined the people's party and was henceforth known as Lorenzo de Popolano.

Amerigo had been in the employ of "the Magnificent" in Paris, but he, unlike Guido Antonio, was not drawn to either party. He felt neutral for he could see that both had good and bad policies. He also realized that Lorenzo, the Magnificent, was now assuming more of the power of a dictator. Amerigo's uncle, Giorgio, who despised dictatorship, was turning away from him. After considering Lorenzo de Popolano's offer, Amerigo decided to take the job. He moved into the Popolano's villa and became a prosperous merchant.

On a business trip to Pisa he was able to purchase a map that would help him pursue his interest in geography. The map cost one hundred thirty gold ducats, which was a big price for the ordinary Florentine citizen. It was "no geographical curiosity", but a practical navigation chart. It had been made by Gabriel de Valesca, a Mallorcan, in the year 1439, and was a map of great accuracy concerning the Mediterranean area. Those were the waters Valesca knew best and at that time were the waters most important for navigation.

Amerigo and his uncle, Giorgio Antonio, both studied the map with interest. They were well aware that ocean travel was becoming more important. They had both been disciples of Toscanelli and his death renewed their interest in the idea that since the world was round, the Indies could be reached by sailing west as well as by sailing to the east. Toscanelli's letter written in 1474, to the Canon of the Cathedral in Lisbon, was remembered by them. This letter, no doubt, was to have a direct influence on the discovery of America by Columbus. Ten years later when Amerigo was in Seville he was to recall that Columbus too had heard about the contents of this letter and had written to Toscanelli to inquire about it. Toscanelli replied by sending him a copy of it which no doubt helped him persuade Queen Isabella to grant him permission for his famous voyage. Columbus was to keep this letter carefully the rest of his life. It was highly prized by him, and is still extant and is in the famous library collection of Columbus's younger son, Ferdinand. The letter in part is quoted below:

. . . I am happy to learn of the friendship of your serene and magnificent king that you enjoy; and in as much as I have often discussed with you the shortest sea route from here to The Indies, where the spices are found, which is much shorter than the route you now use via Guinea and you tell me His Highness would like me to give him some clarification or proof . . . I could demonstrate this to him globe in hand . . . facing this line to the west the beginning of India is drawn . . . and travelling leagues (west) you will reach marvelously fertile lands with every kind of spice and gems and precious stones. And do not wonder that I speak of the West, referring to the land where spices grow, which is commonly said to be in the East; for those who sail steadily west will find that region to the west and those who travel eastward overland will find them in the east . . . "

Just as it was in Spain and Portugal, the guiding thought in the

Florence of the fifteenth century was the hope for a new route to the Orient. Florence's mercantile business was suffering since the Turks had captured Constantinople. Not only did they charge exorbitant rates for the mercantile caravans crossing their domain, often outlaw Turks stole the goods outright and killed the travelers. Egypt now, too, had become a part of the great Moslem Turk holdings known as Ottoman Empire and travel via the Red Sea to the Indian Ocean was under the Turk's control. The once lucrative trade with the Orient was no longer lucrative.

Both Giorgio and Amerigo thought Toscanelli theories were plausible and possible. The study of Valesca's map excited them but they realized that ocean travel would be quite different. They recalled Old Amerigo's words "the world is changing" and the future of the mercantile business would turn to the great Ocean Sea, but since their life in Florence was pleasant though uneventful, they were not anxious to leave their native city.

Giorgio's reputation as a scholar was growing. He had been tonsured and was in line for a bishopric. The presence of Guido Antonio at the Vatican was helping him.

Just as he had been successful with the mission in France, Guido was also succeeding with Pope Sextus IV. The Pope was anxious, again, to be on good terms with Florence. He had turned away from political ambition and was now interested in decorating the Sistine Chapel, and it is for this his name is mostly remembered. He turned to Guido Antonio, who was then the ambassador from Florence, for he knew of Florence's devotion to art. Guido suggested two Florentine artists, Sandro Botticelli and Ghirlandaio. Both painted for the Vespucci family and both had been recently commissioned to paint frescos for the Vespucci chapel in Ognissanti, Botticelli to paint St. Augustine and Ghirlandaio to paint St. Jerome. It was agreed that if the Pope liked the chapel paintings, they would be commissioned to come to Rome.

The subtitle for Botticelli painting was St. Augustine in Toscanelli's study and in the background is an astrolabe and an armillary sphere. Giorgio had obtained the astrolabe for the painting and both he and Amerigo studied its use. These frescos with the one of the Vespucci family can be seen in Ognissanti today. In the family portrait Simonetta Vespucci, Amerigo's cousin, represents the Virgin with the boy, Amerigo, and the monk is Giorgio to one side.

Pope Sextus liked the frescos, so Botticelli and Ghirlandaio were invited to Rome to paint frescos in the Sistine Chapel. Botticelli painted the leper who had been healed by Jesus and Ghirlandaio painted the scene of Jesus calling St. Peter and St. Andrew to be his disciples. In the background of both pictures are crowds of Romans and Florentines. The faces of them are of the artist's contemporaries. In one corner Ghirlandaio painted a handsome picture of Guido Antonio Vespucci. Michelangelo would later be summoned from Florence to Rome to paint the famous ceiling of the chapel.

For the next ten years Amerigo was busy in the employ of Lorenzo di Pier Francisco de Medici. Often he was sent to Seville for it was there that ocean trade was flourishing. The trade on the Mediterranean was seriously declining and soon it was clear that Spain was the place for the mercantile business and Lorenzo asked Amerigo to go there permanently.

"What?" he answered, "Leave Florence?"

"At least think about it, Amerigo," replied Lorenzo "I have a wife and children so I can't go."

"I just never thought of leaving Florence. Short trips are fine, but it is just something I have never considered. I'll think about it," answered Amerigo.

Chapter XI

Amerigo Decides to Go to Spain

It was the year 1491. This was the year Amerigo decided to leave Florence to make his home in Spain. He was almost forty years old, a rather unusual age to make a new beginning, but the declining importance of Florence in the banking and mercantile business made the change necessary. His immediate concern in Spain would be in outfitting ships for ocean voyages, but finally he would go to sea.

As a trading center, Florence had in the early years forged ahead of Italy's sea coast cities. It was strategically located on the important north-south trade routes from Naples and Rome to Bologna and on to Milan. Venice, Genoa, and Pisa competed for the rich Mediterranean trade from the Orient and Florence was in easy reach of each. Also she was in the middle of a rich farming area and being an inland city was safer from plundering pirates so the papacy deposited the large sums of money brought by pilgrims in Florence banks.

Now, the center for trade was moving west. No longer was the Mediterranean and its seaports able to monopolize the rich trade from the Orient. Gold had been discovered in Guinea. The Canary Islands had been rediscovered. Daring sailors were gradually making the great Ocean Sea the place for trading ships. For centuries ships had hugged the shore afraid to venture in the open water. That fear of the ocean was vanishing and trade was shifting to Portugal and Spain, particularly Seville. Amerigo was aware of these changes so he was not surprised when asked to go permanently to Spain. Still he had never really faced the problem. Now he had to make the big decision.

It had often been said that the worst punishment except death that could be inflicted on a Florentine was being banished from his native city. "Now," Amerigo mused. "It seems I must banish myself."

That night he lay awake thinking, "Shall I leave Florence? I, now, have no family responsibilities to keep me here. Mona Lisa has joined Old Stagio in heaven. Girolamo has returned from the Holy Land and has entered the San Marco Monastery. He teaches Latin there so he is settled. Bernardo," he continued to muse, "I guess is still somewhere in Hungary. If he returns to Florence, I'll have Antonio suggest that he join me in Spain. That might appeal to his adventurous spirit. Yes, I'll talk to Antonio tonight. Catarina has asked me to come have dinner with them. Now, it will be hard to leave Antonio and his family, especially the children. I guess I will miss Giovanni the most. We have been very close."

"And Florence is changing," Amerigo continued to muse. "Lorenzo is too ill to take care of the affairs of state and his son, Pietro, seems to lack the leadership qualities of his father and grandfathers. Even if he possessed that wisdom and ability that monk Savonarola by his Old Testament preachings and charades against Lorenzo has divided Florence into two opposing parties. Even my family is on different sides, Guido Antonio sides with Lorenzo the Magnificent and Uncle Giorgio is leaning toward Savonarola. He must be preaching more effectively than I think. Maybe I should go to hear him preach tomorrow, I will go with Giorgio to the Cathedral before I make up my mind."

The next morning he and his Uncle Giorgio were in the Cathedral for the eleven o'clock service. When Savonarola stepped to the pulpit, there was a quiet expectancy in the great room. The monk began to speak with a persuasive voice.

"God wants to make you happy and he wants to give you a head, a king, who will govern you and that is Christ. What are these shows, these vile festivals of Lorenzo's. They are the work of a despot. Why does Lorenzo put them on?" the shrill voice of Savonarola paused. The audience waited breathlessly. Then he continued, "He puts them on to amuse the people so he can rule as a tyrant."

Savonarola then held up a small Greek statute in one hand and a small Roman statute in the other. "These are shameless displays of naked men and women idolizing heathen gods. Is this beauty? You women who glory in your ornaments and your hair! Are you beautiful? No, you are ugly! I tell you. Enter the Duomo (Cathedral). Look at the women and men in prayer. There you will see true beauty, the beauty of God shining in their faces as in the face of an angel.

When the service was over; the two men walked slowly through the doors of the Cathedral into the sunshine outside. Their faces were sad and their mood was not cheered by the sunshine. As they began their short walk back toward the Vespucci home, Amerigo said, "What is going to happen in Florence? Lorenzo may die soon.

What then?"

"It will not be a happy time," agreed Giorgio.

"But why, Uncle Giorgio," asked Amerigo, " Are you condoning Savonarola? He seems to be a reckless demigod. He is not preaching what you have taught me; he is not preaching the Christian way but with Old Testament words he is threatening the people with the fires of hell. He is making the women weep and strong men shiver. Children are bewildered."

"Yes, Amerigo, I understand all that. I am not blindly following him. I heartily disapprove of the way he is using our children to spy on their parents," said Giorgio.

"I know that since the Pazzi Conspiracy, Lorenzo has assumed almost dictatorial power, but what kind of government will Florence have with Savonarola. He, too, probably will be a dictator," said Amerigo.

"Perhaps," retorted his uncle sadly. "Perhaps the pendulum will swing too far."

"You, Uncle Giorgio, made me believe in Aristotle's golden means that too much of anything is wrong," said Amerigo.

"Yes," agreed Giorgio, "and Savonarola is likely to push to the other extreme. We hope, however, to persuade him to turn back to our old democracy, to give the vote back to the people. As it is now too few Florentines have the power to vote and today, the strong oppress the weak, the rich stamp on the poor."

"But I don't believe that Savonarola will ever be reasonable," said Amerigo.

"Again I say, you may be right," said his uncle. "We hope that Savonarola's harsh ways will be moderated and we hope again to have a fairer government."

"It is my hope, too, but who would head up such a government?" asked Amerigo.

"You may be sure surprised to know that it is your friend and my former student, Piero Soderini. He is now in the Signoria, you know," said Giorgio.

"But, Uncle, Piero would never go along with a fanatic like Savonarola. That, I'm sure of," exclaimed Amerigo.

"You may be right," agreed Giorgio. "It is a big gamble but one thing is sure. Florence will change after Lorenzo's death. We can just hope to change it for the better."

They reached the steps of the old Vespucci house. "Come, shall we go in," Giorgio suggested.

"No, not until I hear what you think about my departing Florence and going to Seville. You must advise me for you are the wisest person I know," said Amerigo earnestly. "Seville is fast taking Florence's place as the center for trade."

"Yes, I know, our Florence is declining and Seville is emerging as the trade center. A man must go where his business takes him," said Giorgio.

"So you agree," said Amerigo gratefully. "Your opinion will

make it easier for me to decide."

"Amerigo, you have been like a son to me and I will miss you sorely. Nevertheless, I advise you to go. A new era for the world is unfolding and you must be part of it," replied Giorgio. "But come, we must go in. Catarina will be expecting us."

"You go ahead, Giorgio and tell Catarina that I will be back in time for dinner. Now, I need time to walk and think and make up my mind," said Amerigo.

The two parted. Giorgio climbed the stone steps and at the door turned to look at Amerigo sadly. Amerigo had turned his steps in the directions of the old clock tower in the Piazza del Signoria. Soon he changed directions and made his way to the Dominican Monastery of San Marco. "I was fortunate to have Uncle Giorgio as my teacher. Savonarola is head master now. I wonder what kind of education the boys of Florence are receiving from him. Is he teaching them to despise the beautiful paintings in San Marco? He even lives in one of the cells decorated by the beautiful frescos of Fra Angelico. There is no spot in Florence more peaceful and beautiful than San Marco," he mused.

Amerigo, then moved slowly on to the nearby Franciscan Church of Santa Croce. He went inside to again admire the frescos of Giotto. He lit a candle and kneeled to pray for Florence and to ask for God's guidance.

He walked on past the great dome of the Cathedral Santo Maria del Fiore and paused to admire the graceful bell tower, which was also designed by Giotto. "I believe Giotto is my favorite artist," he mused, but as he walked on he paused to admire the east door of the Baptistery. "But Ghiberti's work is so beautiful, too, both were masters. Ghiberti was only twenty-four when he carved them."

"This is my Florence and I'm leaving it. Yes," he said finally to himself. "I'm leaving it to go to Seville. My mind is made up."

He thought of Dante who had been banished and always dreamed of returning but was never allowed to.

"I will be able to return whenever I wish," he told himself. "That thought made him more comfortable about his resolve to leave.

Spain, however, and fate had different plans for Amerigo. He never returned to Florence except for brief visits.

Finally he found himself in the Piazza del Signoria. He looked at the old clock tower and his thoughts went back to that long ago festival time when he was only sixteen. It seemed only yesterday that he was dancing with the lovely Elena. Suddenly he looked up and found himself again looking into merry brown eyes. "Elena! Elena!" he gasped.

"No," said the owner of the merry brown eyes. "I am not Elena but she has sent you a message."

"Elena, where is she? You must tell me," he begged earnestly.

"Elena is dead," the young woman continued. "She asked me to come tell you."

"But you, you are so much like her!" exclaimed Amerigo.

"I'm Elena's daughter," she said, and after a brief pause, "and yours!"

"Mine!" exclaimed Amerigo. "It couldn't be."

"But it is true," she replied and held up the golden locket he had given Elena. "My name is also Elena and this is my daughter and your granddaughter."

Amerigo stood speechless, looking down at the little three year old. He finally collected himself and said, "Come let us find a place where we can talk."

Amerigo led them to a nearby bench in the Piazza. He stooped down and looked intently at the little girl, and then reached into his pocket and pulled out a lollipop, one that he had planned to give to Antonio's youngest. The child timidly took the lollipop and looked at her mother. "You can eat it, but don't forget to say thank you," her mother reminded her.

The child looked up at Amerigo and said in a soft voice, "I like you."

"That is a nice way to say thank you," he said gravely. He beckoned her to sit and he sat beside her never taking his eyes off the tiny child.

"All this is difficult for me to comprehend. I am sad to think of all that I have missed. I want you to know that Elena meant a lot to me and has never been far from my thoughts throughout the years," said Amerigo softly.

"And memories of you also lingered for Elena all of her life. When we came through Florence, she would inquire about you. She thought that it was best to remain out of your life," she said.

"Tell me more about her," begged Amerigo.

"She had a gypsy husband who was a good father to me. He, too, is now dead," disclosed the young woman.

"Then," said Amerigo eagerly, "You and the little child must come with me to Seville. I plan to leave in a fortnight."

His daughter, the second Elena said soberly, "No, I am a gypsy like my Mother. I, too, have a good gypsy husband."

But seeing the sadness in Amerigo's face quickly added, "Our chief has said that next winter we may winter in Spain. Perhaps we will see you then."

Amerigo gently took the little girl into his arms and held her close. The child looked up at him and smiled.

"I have missed a lot," he confessed to his daughter.

Elena quietly put her arms around Amerigo and whispered, "I'm sure you would have been a good father."

They sat silently for a while. The clock in the tower struck five. "It is getting late. We must go," she stated.

"Wait, a bit. Let us go to a nearby goldsmith shop so I can buy little Elena a locket," he pleaded.

Together they walked to the shop on the nearby Ponte Vecchio and Amerigo made the purchase and gave it to Elena. She put the locket around her daughter's neck. The child held it up and admired it and thanked him with a little smile.

Amerigo stood silently as he watched until they were out of sight. "I have missed a lot," he repeated. "Yes, I have missed a lot!" he said to himself as he slowly turned toward the Vespucci home. "Elena dead," he thought sadly. "She was so young and gay. She probably made her gypsy husband a good wife. And her daughter, our daughter is so much like her. Yes, I have missed a lot."

Chapter XII

Columbus Discovers America

It was 1492, a very important year for Spain and for the world. Early in 1492, Queen Isabella and King Ferdinand had succeeded in capturing Granada, the last stronghold of the Moors and had driven them out of Spain. The sovereign then gave permission to Columbus to make his famous voyage, the voyage that changed the geography of the world. It opened up the ocean and another hemisphere for exploration and colonization. It also opened up men's minds and freed them of long held myths and superstitions.

It was also the year Amerigo left Florence and came to Seville in Spain to look after the Medici mercantile business. Seville, because of Columbus's great discovery, would become the center for World trade and would remain the busiest port for more than a century. Seville, like Florence in Italy, was located close to a large agricultural region. All the farm products, the wine and the olive oil as well as the silk from Toledo and Grenada were sent to Seville for export. Seville was also the home of many nobles and wealthy merchants. They financed many of the great voyages.

Amerigo was lucky, too, because at that time Italian sailors and merchants were especially welcome in Spain. Maritime business was shifting from the Mediterranean to the great Ocean Sea. The discovery of gold on the African coast by the Portuguese and their rounding of the Cape of Good Hope by Bartholomew Diaz had proved that ocean voyages were not only possible but now would be profitable. The Italian sailors and merchants because they had sailed the Mediterranean were considered more experienced and canny, and Amerigo was a merchant. As he sailed up the Guadalquiver River on the last leg of his journey from Florence to Seville, he saw hundreds of ships anchored along its shores. They flew the flags of many nations.

"No wonder Bernardi needs help," he mused, "the number of ships in the harbor has more than doubled since I was here last year. There will be plenty to keep me busy. I won't have time to pine for Florence."

Amerigo's first glimpse of Seville was of the great, golden, eight sided tower, the Torre del Oro. In the bright Andulasian sunlight with the mighty Alcazar fortress palace in the background, it was indeed a magnificent sight.

"Seville gives one a golden welcome," he thought. "I am looking forward to my stay here" and his stay in Seville did prove longer and more pleasant than he had ever expected.

When the ship docked, Amerigo made his way to Bernardi's place of business on the bank of the river. Bernardi, like Amerigo, was a Florentine. He had come to Seville years ago and was well established in the mercantile business that financed and outfitted ships and since he had been handling the Medici business for more than a year, he was no stranger to Amerigo. He and Bernardi had worked closely together and as the maritime business was increasing, he had asked for Amerigo's full-time help.

Bernardi greeted Amerigo warmly and said, " You are welcome. By all the ships in the harbor, you can understand why you are needed. Come, I have arranged for you to have quarters in my home if that's agreeable with you. I will need you to be close by."

"It will be fine with me," answered Amerigo. "You are very thoughtful."

"Since my wife's death, my daughter, Luisa, keeps house for me. Come and meet her and her husband. "Luisa," he called as they entered the large Spanish villa, "Amerigo is here."

Soon a young woman appeared, followed by her Spanish husband. "Welcome to Seville," she said as she extended her hand. "It is good to have you come to help father. He has been working late and early as you probably have heard, and in Spain, one likes some leisure time for siestas. I am Luisa and this is my husband, Pedro."

"I, too, want to welcome you to Seville," said Pedro warmly. "Seville is now a busy city, but remains an interesting place."

"Yes, Amerigo, we are proud of Seville. You must go with us tonight to let the city welcome you," added Luisa.

"Thank-you, it will be my pleasure. I am anxious to get acquainted with Seville for I expect to be here for some time," answered Amerigo.

"But you must be weary," said Luisa. "Come and I will show

you to your room."

She led Amerigo to a room opening off the patio. "I hope you will be comfortable here," she added.

"I am sure I will be," he answered as be looked around the pleasant room. An orange tree was in full bloom outside on the patio and the sweet perfume had seeped into the room.

That evening, Amerigo walked with Bernardi, Luisa and Pedro to the town. On the way, Luisa explained, "In Spain, we have a gay custom. At sundown all the young people take a walk around the plaza. The young men walk in one direction and the young women walked in the opposite direction. When the two groups meet, the young man asks the first young woman that he meets for the first dance. It is a merry way to start the evening and I hope you will join in the fun!"

"But I'm not a young man," protested Amerigo.

"But you are unmarried," Luisa responded quickly, "and that qualifies you. Please!" she added.

"All right," Amerigo smiled at her earnestness. "I'll join in the fun."

When they reached the plaza, the young people were already assembling for the Paseo for that was what the walk was called. Amerigo was busy looking around. He had just spotted the graceful bell tower and started toward it, but Luisa caught his arm and pushed him into the group of young men. He joined them with a smile.

As the young men walked, they joked with each other.

Amerigo walked along in silence, listening to the others. Soon the young women came into view.

"They are lovely," he thought, as he watched the colorful group approaching, "but I'm sure they won't compare with our Florentine ladies."

Suddenly he found himself looking into two sparkling brown eyes and he wasn't so sure about the Florentine ladies.

The owner of the eyes looked steadfastly into his, and asked gaily, "Will you have this dance with me?"

"Why, certainly," the astonished Amerigo said as he took her proffered arm. Soon they were dancing to the lively guitar music.

"You must be new in town," the young woman inquired as they danced.

"Yes," Amerigo confessed, "but already I'm beginning to like Seville.

When the music stopped, Luisa quickly walked up to the dancers, and said laughingly, "Amerigo, this is my friend, Maria Cerezo. I have to confess that I arranged this way for you two to meet. I hope you will be friends."

Bernardi and Pedro soon joined them and they went to a nearby cafe. After a leisurely meal, Bernardi said "Amerigo and I will have a busy day tomorrow and I'm sure he needs some sleep in a real bed after his long voyage from Florence, so will you folks excuse us?"

"We have all had a long day," agreed Luisa, "so we, too, will go with you. Come Maria, and we will walk you home."

"Thank you," replied Maria, "that will be nice."

They walked the short distance to Maria's house. "Good night," said Maria to the group and then turning to Amerigo said, "Thank you for the dance."

"It was a pleasant way to start my life in Seville," responded Amerigo. "I will look forward to many more such dances and I will look forward to seeing you again."

"Luisa and I often visit each other so I'm sure we will," replied Maria.

"And maybe Maria and I will show you Seville when you have the time," returned Luisa.

On the way back to the Bernardi home, Luisa explained, "Maria is a widow. Her husband was a sailor. He was lost at sea about five years ago. I hope you will be friends. She has grieved over her loss too long."

"Maria is a good dancer. I find her interesting and I will enjoy seeing more of her," replied Amerigo.

The next morning Amerigo was awake at sun rise. He had slept well his first night in Seville. Soon he and Bernardi had a cup of black coffee and were on their way to Bernardi's business house on the bank of the Guadalquiver River. Despite the early hour they found much activity there.

Soon they were busy. A shipment of salt to the Medici of

Florence must be arranged. Another ship must be outfitted for a voyage to Guinea on the African coast. It was mid morning before the two men found time to pause for breakfast. They walked to a nearby cafe for wine and cheese.

"Amerigo," observed Bernardi, while they were sipping their wine, "you will be interested to know that last August a voyage to the Indies was begun by sailing to the west as your Toscanelli suggested."

"That is especially interesting to me. Have you heard from it? Has he returned?" inquired Amerigo, much interested. "My uncle, Giorgio Antonio, and I have long agreed that such a voyage was possible. Tell me more."

"It is a long story," explained Bernardi. "Many months have passed and we have not heard from him. He, too, was an Italian named Cristobal Colon (Christopher Columbus). I first met him in 1485. He had come to Spain to seek permission and ships for the voyage. He did not get permission until after the sovereign had rid the country of the Moors."

"Cristobal Colon!" said Amerigo. "I heard of him years ago when my uncle and I were visiting in the villa of a learned mathematician. We were interested in a map that he and Toscanelli were making. They were leading scientist and firmly believed that it was possible to reach the Indies by sailing to the West."

"Yes, I know, Colon told me about them. Toscanelli was well known in Portugal. He was the one who suggested to Prince Henry, the Navigator, that sailing south of the equator along the coast of Africa was possible. Toscanelli was a friend of the Canon of the Cathedral in Lisbon and wrote to him suggesting that since he had "the ear of the king" to tell him that he firmly believed the Indies could be reached by sailing directly west. Colon heard about the letter and wrote to Toscanelli who in reply sent him a copy of the letter and also a map," finished Bernardi.

"You knew this Colon!" exclaimed Amerigo.

"Yes," replied Bernardi, "and after being refused permission and ships from the King of Portugal, he came to Spain," Bernardi replied.

"But that was many years ago," returned Amerigo. "I was just a young man when I heard about Colon."

"No doubt, for after being turned down by Portugal, he came to Spain to seek help. Queen Isabella was interested but the sovereigns were too busy trying to drive the Moors out of Spain and were also short of money. They kept putting Colon off. He followed the court around Spain for almost seven years. This Colon was a determined man," concluded Bernardi.

"And after the Moors were expelled, they gave permission for the voyage?" inquired Amerigo.

"Yes, but even then they were short of money. Much of the money and some of the ships were offered from private parties or borrowed. I helped finance the voyage. More than eighty thousand maravedis! Do you, Amerigo, believe such a voyage is possible?" questioned Bernardi.

"Not only do I think it is possible, but many others in Florence do also. How long did you say Colon had been gone?"

"About six or seven months now," replied Bernardi.

"That is a long time but the Indies are on the other side of the world," said Amerigo thoughtfully.

"Colon estimated the distance to be only 2400 miles. If that distance was right, he should have returned by now, don't you think?" asked Bernardi.

"Perhaps Colon figured wrong," declared Amerigo. "And remember Marco Polo was detained in the Great Sinus for years. Don't give up hope yet."

After returning to work, Amerigo asked the sailors about Colon's voyage.

"He's sailed over the side of the world," said one. "We'll never see him or his three ships again."

"He's in the 'land of missing ships'," declared another.

"The King of Portugal was too wise to sponsor such a voyage," exclaimed a third.

As for the old time sailors, most had long given up hope for Colon's (Columbus's) return. Amerigo was so busy the next few weeks that he too almost forgot Columbus. Ships had to be outfitted for shipment of supplies to the Canaries and ports along the African coast also ships to France, and even as far away as England. Very little time was given to leisurely dinners and since it was Lent, there were no dances but every Sunday found Amerigo with his new friends, Bernardi, Luisa, Pedro and Maria, dressed in their Sunday best, having dinner in one of the many cafes.

The ones along the narrow, pedestrian street named Sierpes

were among the ones the five liked most and it was to one of them they went on special occasions.

"Sierpes means snake, doesn't it," queried Amerigo. "How did it get such a name?"

"It is long, narrow and crooked like a snake, hence its name," disclosed Maria.

"I've heard," joined in Luisa, " that it got its name from a picture of a serpent in front of this very cafe."

"No matter," rejoined Pedro. "It is a pleasant place to go for a Sunday dinner and it is especially lively after Easter."

"And during Easter week, the parade of the virgins comes down this street," stated Bernardi. "That is a sight worth seeing."

"Amerigo, you must not miss that," agreed Maria.

So life in Seville, although busy, was made pleasant by these dinners. "Seville has captivated me," Amerigo mused as he returned home that night. "I must write to Uncle Giorgio and tell him about my new life and my new friends."

Seville, 1492

Greetings to my most honorable Uncle,

You will be pleased to know that I arrived safely in Seville and am comfortably situated with quarters in the Villa of Giantto Bernardi. He is the person who handles the Medici business in Seville and I am working with him. He, too, is a Florentine. He has a daughter named Luisa. She and her

Spanish husband have made me welcome.

The first evening after arriving I had dinner with them in the piazza down town. We were joined by Luisa's friend, Maria Cerezo. I found her very pleasant company.

The two ladies both agreed to show me the town. While I had been here before, this time, knowing I will be here for some time, I am exploring the city in depth. The most impressive building is the Cathedral as it is in most towns. It was built on the site of a Muslim mosque and although its exterior is very plain, the interior is magnificent. The cathedral is huge. I believe our Santa Maria del Fiore could be placed inside it and still there would be more room. The aim of the people of Seville as I am told was to build a cathedral that "never should have its equal". Despite its great size, the size is not evident when you go in for its "towering clustered columns" just gives one the feeling of height. It was begun a hundred years ago but yet is not finished.

As beautiful and as large as the cathedral is, it is the adjoining patio that pleased me most. It is known as the Patio de los Naranjos or the Court of the Oranges. It dates back to the time of the mosque and is shaded by rows of orange trees. In the center is a delightful fountain also dating back to the Moors. I understand that merchants conduct their business in this court. I will look forward to that. The fragrance of the orange blossoms is enticing.

Near the cathedral, is a bell tower with bells that toll the hours of the day. It also dates from the Moors and from the top of its inclined stairway one can see all Seville. The ladies and I climbed to the top.

"Now you see our city," exclaimed Maria to me. "Legend has it that Seville was founded by Hercules and enwalled by Julius Caesar." "Aren't you impressed?" she added with a mischievous smile.

Seville is a beautiful city but still I think Giotto's tower in Florence is lovelier and despite the size of the cathedral it does not have the beauty of our Santa Maria del Fiore.

It is the gardens with the colorful and sweet smelling blossoms that set Seville apart from Florence. Rose gardens are abundant and I am assured that jasmine, gardenias and other sweet smelling flowers perfume the air in the springtime and throughout most of the year. Oleanders line the streets.

There are almond trees, fig trees, cork trees and sweet chestnut trees, so along with an abundance of oranges, I can look forward to much delicious fruit.

Another colorful part of Seville is the azulejos tiles. They, too, set the city apart from Florence. They adorn almost every building. The Tower of Gold in the harbor is made golden by them but many azulejos are blue and all other colors on other buildings. These tiles have been made for centuries in a pottery across the river from Seville in the town of Triana.

Triana is also where many sailors live. I probably will spend much time there talking with them. Triana will be especially interesting to me right after Easter for I understand that many gypsies come there for the winter. They have become famous as horse traders. As you know I have long had an interest in gypsies.

In all the large Spanish cities, the Moors built a fortress-palace called the Alcazar. The one in Seville stands on the Seville side of the Guadalquiver River. It is the home of the Spanish kings when they bring the court to Seville and has been used by them for centuries. Interestingly, the Moors were driven out of Cordoba and Seville by Ferdinand III in 1248 and it remained in Spanish hands even though the Moors remained strong elsewhere.

The Alcazar was restored to all its splendor by Pedro the Cruel in 1364. He and his mistress made it their main residence. I understand that his mistress, Maria Padilla, was a very beautiful and fascinating woman. In the basement of the palace is an azulejo decorated vault in which this beautiful woman is said to have bathed. Legend has it that the gallants of Don Pedro's court used to drink her bath water in homage. One, it is said, refused to drink declaring, "If I tasted the sauce, I might covet the porridge."

Maria was buried by Pedro in the Great Cathedral, which shows her status as a mistress.

The Alcazar has an "uncounted" number of rooms, patios and gardens and again it was the gardens that attracted me the most. Here are perfumed orange groves, palm trees, roses and brick walks shaded by box hedges and myrtle. They are delightful.

The eight sided tower that I mentioned earlier stands to one side of the Alcazar. It is rightly called Torre de Oro for the golden azulejos tiles. It is used as a prison and is said to have been kept full during the reign of Pedro the Cruel.

But I'm sure you have heard enough about Seville for now, at least to know that I am captivated by the city and am looking forward to my life here.

How are you? I feel that I abandoned you and Florence in uncertain times. I will be interested to know how Lorenzo is and the happenings there. Is Savonarola still gaining power? Is Lorenzo's death eminent? I will be looking forward to hearing from you and now I bid farewell to my honored uncle and beg him to salute all members of my family in my behalf.

Respectfully yours,
Amerigo

Florence, 1492

To my worthy nephew, Amerigo Vespucci,

It was good to hear that you were well situated in Seville. I passed your nice letter on to Antonio and his family and he, in turn, sent it on to Guido Antonio, who is still in Rome.

The family is fine but our Florence is a sad place since Lorenzo's death. He died on the fortnight after Easter. The French were on our borders, Piero met them at the gates, panicked, and surrendered. The people were furious and banished Piero and all the rest of the Medici except your Popolano. Savonarola took charge and somehow managed to keep the French from sacking Florence by compromising with Charles II.

A short time later, when Savonarola was firmly in control, he built a large bonfire on the Piazza Signoria and commanded all the people to come burn what he called "their vanities", their jewels, their furs, their fine clothes and some books that he considered blasphemous. It was sad to see so much beauty go up in smoke. I must confess to you, that you were right about your friend, Piero Soderini. He refused to accept Savonarola's type of government and we are no closer to a democracy than we were under Lorenzo. Savonarola calls his government the "dictatorship of God." People are frightened. They are afraid they will be damned if they disobey him or fail to obey his dictatorial laws and to think I was naive enough to help him come to power.

Again, we realize the wisdom of Aristotle's golden means; we were seeking moderation, Lorenzo had become a tyrant after the Pazzi affair and Savonarola is also a tyrant in the name of religion.

Now that Savonarola is in power, the people in Florence seldom laugh heartily and if one dares smile, it was usually a wan one. Yes, we still have some festivals and celebrations but usually they are solemn as funerals. Only Church music is played. No dancing is permitted in the streets. Now Savonarola has everything his way. No one dares cross him for fear of being damned.

Even the children are subdued. They make up a large part of the parades, all dressed in white and piously marching in procession carrying lighted candles.

As you probably know, the Popolano Medici were not banished but their business is depressed as are most other businesses.

Savonarola has been summoned to Rome by Pope Alexander VI, but refuses to go. He even calls for Alexander to step down, branding him as a priest of the devil.

I am glad you are in Spain for Florence is not the same. You escaped just in time. It must be very different in Seville. I will be waiting anxiously to hear more of what is happening there. Has Cristobal Colon returned?

Antonio and Catarina send you their regards and best wishes and wish me to advise you that Giovanni is still anxious to join you in Seville. We will look forward to hearing from you. It's good to know you are well and are finding life there pleasant. We sincerely pray that Colon will return safely. It would have pleased Toscanelli very much if his theory proves to be correct. It is sad that he did not live to know about this wonderful undertaking.

Your devoted uncle and friend,
Giorgio Antonio

Chapter XIII

Columbus's Return from his Famous Voyage

It was the year 1493. This was the year Columbus returned from his famous voyage, the voyage that opened up travel to the west by the great Ocean Sea. It would put Spain and especially Seville on the road to riches and power. It would change the geography and the history of the world. Amerigo would be a part of this exciting age.

He and Bernardi were busy when word came from Palos that Columbus had returned. The news was received by the sailors and all Seville with thankfulness and joy. At last Spain had succeeded in achieving what Lisbon had not been able to do, a western water way to the Indies!

Columbus had stopped in Lisbon for ship repairs and from there had dispatched his now famous letter telling Queen Isabella and King Ferdinand that he reached the Indies on October 12, 1492. He sent second copy to them from Palos and a third to his mistress Beatriz in Cordoba. He reached the little port of Palos, at midday on March 15, 1493, 224 days after sailing from there. To rest up he spent two weeks with his special friend, Fray Juan Perez, in the monastery at Rabida.

It was Fray Perez who had helped him get an audience with the sovereigns when he first came to Spain. Perez remained a loyal friend during his period of waiting for ships and permission to sail.

Columbus arrived in Seville on Palm Sunday. By that time the great news of his return had been wide spread. He had become a celebrity. As his ship sailed up the Guadalquiver River, crowds were on hand to welcome him. It was a fitting welcome for the man whose voyage forever altered the maps of the world. A New Hemisphere had been discovered.

Bernardi and Amerigo were among the crowd that greeted Columbus. As soon as he could get away from his well-wishing friends, he turned to Bernardi and said, "Bernardi, you believed in me and now, I want to ask other favors of you. On the ship I have the men that I brought from the Indies. Will you keep them for me until I am summoned by the Sovereign? I also have exotic birds that must be cared for? Will you also look after them for me?"

"Certainly," agreed Bernardi. "It will be an honor to be of service to you and now Colon, I want you to meet my co-worker, Amerigo Vespucci. He is also from Italy."

It was then that Columbus and Amerigo met, the two men who became friends in life but who, after their death would become the focus of a bitter controversy that would last for centuries. It was their voyages and their writings that would excite Europe and send map makers back to their drawing boards.

At a word from Columbus, the "strange men and even stranger birds" were brought on deck. The crowd gasped in astonishment. They were of a reddish-brown color and completely naked. It took some time for the excitement to die down, so the men and birds could be unloaded. The poor savages were being treated like cargo, as were the gaily colored parrots but soon all were quartered in Bernardi's warehouse.

One of Spain's eminent historians, Bartholome de Las Casas, who was a mere lad at the time wrote much later this eloquent description of them.

"I saw them in Seville. Those who could fathom the inner recesses of the heart can try to figure out what went on in their souls, if they had souls__ of those poor devils, or in the senses__ and those they had and keen, ___ of those innocents. Their tongues being useless, they were all eyes. Until a few months before their world, like their fathers and their fathers' fathers before them had been the rustling trees, the restless sea, the fiery sun, the coconut fleshed moon. A strange man had come out of the sea and had taken them prisoner, had put them in huge ships with sails of cloth, which danced on the waves of the sea. They ran into the worst storm the sailors had ever seen and before they reached Portugal the Atlantic was like the Caribbean in the hurricane season. The Indians had never experienced a hurricane on the high seas. The pitching of the ships made them sick unto death. And when they had come through that, Columbus handled them like an animal trainer. The world seemed to be turned into a hand with a thousand fingers, all eager to touch their flesh, eyes examining their teeth and scrutinizing their rear for a tail that was not there. Even in the still of the night, they hardly dared talk to one another. Their only escape, their only flight, was to huddle together, to touch each other as though they formed a single cluster of human flesh. The only moment of relief was when sleep overpowered them and then what nightmare must have ridden them."

Bartholome de las Casas, who wrote this moving description, was to become a monk and spend many years seeking to lessen the plight of these natives. He also wrote a history of this period and a biography of Columbus.

Shortly after Easter, the eagerly awaited letter from Queen Isabella and King Ferdinand commanding Columbus to attend the Royal Court in Barcelona. The letter was addressed to "Don Cristobal Colon, our Admiral of the Ocean Sea and Governor of the islands that he hath discovered in the Indies." This was the exact title that Columbus had insisted upon. The letter continued "in as much as we will that which you have commenced with the aid of God be continued and forwarded, we have ordered preparations for a second voyage."

The long trip to Barcelona was to be overland and preparation had already been made for it. Columbus had purchased the proper clothes for an audience with the sovereigns. He led the procession on horseback. Some of his officers also followed on horseback.

Servants and the Indians walked or rode along in wagons. Only six of the ten Indians were well enough to make the journey. They wore a loin cloth for modesty's sake and were decked out with feathered headgear. Around their neck hung gold and silver ornaments. They carried cages of the brightly colored parrots. People lined up on the side of the road and cheered as they watched the strange procession.

The cavalcade traveled through Andalusia to Cordoba. There it stopped for a rest, and to greet Beatriz, Columbus's mistress, and to pick up his sons, Diego and Ferdinand, before traveling on to Barcelona.

The procession reached Barcelona in April. The king and queen stood to greet Columbus and gave him a hero's welcome. They then held a Thanksgiving service for God's guidance and for Columbus's safe return. It was the high point in Columbus's life.

Columbus spent three months at the Royal Court while plans were being made for his second voyage. The courtiers courted him and the scholars who before had belittled him now paid him great respect.

The pope was notified of the discovery and the archdeacon of Seville, Don Juan de Fonseca, who then was a friend of Columbus, was ordered to organize a fleet for the second voyage. This gave Columbus a chance to take care of his affairs and time to make a pilgrimage to pay homage to the Virgin of Guadalupe. He had made a solemn vow to do so during the terrible storm that almost caused disaster on his return voyage.

Meanwhile back in Seville, Juan de Fonseca began preparing a large fleet for Columbus's second great voyage. Bernardi was engaged to outfit a 102 tonnage ship and to purchase 203,000 ship biscuits so he and Amerigo were busy. In fact all shipbuilders in the area were busy for seventeen ships had been ordered by the sovereigns.

Many sailors of Columbus's great voyage often gathered to talk about it. Amerigo asked them many questions and was an interested listener. When Columbus returned to Seville often Bernardi, Amerigo, and he got together to talk about the voyage, and often Juan de la Cosa and Bishop Fonseca joined them. They developed a special relationship of respect although they were not always in agreement. They would take a break during a busy day to talk about the use of the compass and the astrolabe. They studied them carefully. Much use of the compass was made by Columbus on his first voyage but he lacked an astrolabe. His great skill in navigation had depended mostly on the compass, the sky, and "dead reckoning".

"The sky seems to have been your most important help in the navigation of your ship?" questioned Amerigo. "Your skill in navigation must be greatly admired. If you had not been such a great navigator the voyage might not have ended so well."

"And it might not have even started without the support of Luis de Santangel of Barcelona," spoke up Columbus quickly. "It was he who not only persuaded the Queen but it was he who guaranteed the maravedis to back the expedition."

"That is true," agreed Fonseca. "But Queen Isabella supported the idea all along. She hesitated because of the lack of funds and don't forget, Columbus, it was you who on this great expedition ventured into the uncharted sea."

"All of that is true, for no success would have been possible without Columbus's grim determination. We were all ready to give up. We pleaded with him to turn back but he stood firm to his purpose. His orders were, "West, nothing to the south, nothing to the north. It was you Columbus that deserves the credit," concluded Juan de la Cosa.

"We all took our chances. It was a combined effort. You, Juan, lost your ship, remember," added Columbus modestly. "But now, Amerigo, I understand that you have an astrolabe. I would like to examine it. Do you think it really helps?"

"I'm sure it will," said Amerigo. "My uncle bought it from Toscanelli's study. I will bring it tomorrow."

"Also," added Columbus, "I want to talk to you more about Toscanelli. No doubt it was his letter that helped me get support for my voyage."

"It will be a pleasure," answered Amerigo. "My uncle knew him well and I much admired and studied both his writings and his map."

"I keep Toscanelli's letter with my most prized possessions," added Columbus. "He was most kind to send me a copy."

"He was interested in your plan and firmly believed in it. I wish he could have lived long enough to know of your famous voyage," sighed Amerigo. "But, now there is a question I would like to ask you two. Why did you ride more than one hundred miles out of your way to pay homage to the Virgin of Guadalupe? There are many virgins right here in Seville. Why did you pick the mountainous shrine?"

Juan de la Cosa was quick to respond, "If you had been with us when the hurricane struck off the coast of the Azores, you would realize that only a miracle saved us from its fury. We were all on our knees praying."

"Then," quickly added Columbus, "I made a vow to go to her shrine. The Virgin of Guadalupe is not an ordinary virgin. She has saved Spain many times."

"Sailors do have to trust in the Divine. We were so thankful when our ship finally rode out the storm that all on board were anxious to acknowledge divine deliverance that we all vowed to go to the first shrine we came to, to offer thanks. And we did," continued Juan, "but it got us into trouble. As soon as we sighted land, we saw a little church. We solemnly stripped to our shirts and proceeded to the church leaving only Columbus and a few on board. We can smile now but then we were a serious group as we knelt to pray. No wonder the locals were skeptical of us. Grown men clad only in their shirts, on their knees at the altar! The Portuguese captain of the island accused us of being an illegal ship bringing slaves from Africa. They threw us into jail," Juan finished his story.

"And it was not easy to persuade this Portuguese Captain to release them. I had to threaten to shoot up the town," recalled Columbus.

"We had some funny experiences," laughed Juan, "and, Columbus, no one seems to have found the message in the bottle that you threw overboard at the height of the storm. If we had been lost at sea, no one would ever have known."

"And just think what Spain and the world would have missed if your ship had not reached shore safely," Amerigo observed seriously. "No one would have dared undertake such a voyage again. Your foresight and daring demand admiration!"

"But as interesting as this conversation has been, we have work to do," broke in Bernardi. "We will have to postpone our talk until another time."

The men returned to work but gathered almost every day in the next few weeks to talk, to study the charts, and to examine the astrolabe. Juan de la Cosa had made charts of the voyage and in the next few years would make many charts and maps of this New World.

Amerigo was still curious about The Lady of Guadalupe, so the next Sunday when he had dinner with Luisa, Pedro, Maria, and Bernardi, he asked, "Tell me about the Virgin of Guadalupe. Why is she so special?"

"She is the most famous virgin in all Spain," responded Maria.

"She is believed to be responsible for many victories over the Moors. Her beginning is also special. Legend has it that she was carved by no other than St. Luke, the author of the third gospel. He was a man of many talents. We mostly hear that he was a physician but he was also an artist. The little Virgin was in a cathedral in Constantinople until the time of the great plague in Italy. Then Pope Gregory, the Great, commanded that she be brought to Rome. She was paraded down the street and the plague vanished."

Pedro added, "And later she was brought to Spain. When the Moors were overrunning Spain in the 700's, she was buried in the remote mountain of Estremadura so she would not be captured. Then her hiding place was forgotten and she remained buried for centuries."

Maria continued, "Many interesting tales are told about how she was found but I guess the most believed one is that when a cowherd was looking for a cow, he saw her head sticking out of the ground. She had been uncovered by the rains, and now a beautiful monastery has been built for her at the spot in which she was found."

"And all kings and queens of Spain have made pilgrimages to her shrine," continued Luisa, anxious to tell what she knew. "She is given credit for our recent driving out the Moors and many Spaniards believe that she can perform miracles."

"She must be quite a lady," observed Amerigo. "Have any of you ever visited her shrine?"

"No," they confessed in unison.

Luisa explained, "The shrine is located in such a remote mountain area that we have not attempted the trip but we all plan to go someday. Maybe, we should plan such a trip."

Later Amerigo wrote the following letter to Florence:

Seville, 1493

To My Honorable Uncle, Giorgio Antonio,

I salute you. It is sad to hear about the conditions in our once happy city. Lorenzo did become a dictator but he was a benevolent one. Savonarola sounds so intolerant. May God in his mercy restore Florence to the kind of Democracy we once enjoyed. I will be anxious to hear further news.

By now, I'm sure you have heard about Columbus's return from his famous voyage westward over the great Ocean Sea. He discovered many islands and he is sure that they are islands off the coast of the Great Sinus. One may be the island of Cipangu. He brought back strange looking natives. They wore no clothes but were completely naked, not even a loin cloth. They do not resemble the natives described by Marco Polo. He also brought fascinating and beautifully colored birds but no spices or any of the rich cloth that one would expect to find in the Orient. The most valuable things he brought back were small gold figures. This excited the people and pleased the sovereigns.

Great preparations were made for another voyage. Bernardi was ordered to outfit one of the ships so we have been busy. They were to be ready in three months. The sovereigns feared that the Portuguese might try to get ahead of them.

Since Bernardi helped finance Columbus's first voyage and because the natives and gaily colored birds were housed in our warehouse, I have had the pleasure and honor of meeting this great sailor. We have had many discussions about his discoveries. I wish you could talk to him.

On September 25, 1493, Columbus set sail on his second voyage. Seventeen ships had been made ready and each flew on her main staff the Royal Standard of Castile. Brightly colored banners waved merrily from each ship, trumpets and drums sounded as this magnificent fleet slowly made its way out of the harbor of Cadiz. This was no doubt the largest fleet that had ever sailed out of any Spanish harbor. It was an impressive sight.

Interestingly enough, nearly all Spain in contrast to the first voyage sought to go on this voyage; even I was tempted. Columbus had his pick. He took about 1200 in all, some seamen, some colonists, as well as men at arms, plus 200 Spanish gentlemen. The purpose is to start a trading post and colony and to continue exploring the area.

A few months have passed since he sailed and twelve of the seventeen vessels have returned. They brought back considerable gold and have reported discovering a gold mine on the island. The gold caused great excitement. Also brought back was a kind of cinnamon and pepper but this proved inferior to that brought from the Indies.

The captain-general of this returning fleet also reported that Columbus had discovered about twenty more large islands. Regular trade is contemplated and we have a busy time ahead of us here in Seville. I must close now but will write more as other events occur.

Keep me posted as to the affairs of Florence. I pray

with you that again our city can be a happy place under a more democratic rule. My regards to Antonio and family and to my brother Girolamo. Nothing has been heard of the venturesome young Bernardi, I judge. May he be well and happy. Tell Antonio that I will welcome Giovanni whenever he will allow him to come. May God be with us all and my special regards to you my respected uncle.

Your admiring nephew,
Amerigo Vespucci

Chapter XIV

Columbus's Second Voyage

It was the year 1494. Columbus's fleet of seventeen vessels had sailed from Cadiz on September 25, 1492. The flagship, the largest, was named the Santa Maria for the one lost on the first voyage. In the fleet were two other large ships, the Colina and the La Gallega, and the small Nina. Ten other square-rigged caravels and several smaller barques for shallow water sailing completed the imposing fleet.

Bernardi and Amerigo had outfitted at least one of the ships. Columbus, for this very important second voyage, planned to found a permanent colony as a base for trading and also to do more exploration. He had no trouble getting volunteers this time. Among these were some who would soon become well-known. There were Ponce de Leon, who was to discover Florida in 1513 and Pedro de las Casas, whose son, Bartholome de las Casas, would become Columbus's biographer. Bartholome also would become the great historian of this glorious era and a champion for better conditions for the Indians. Also on board was Alonso de Ojeda, a daring young soldier with whom Amerigo would sail in 1499. Ojeda had become a favorite of the

Queen because of his daring escapades. He had danced on the topmost ledge of the two hundred foot Giralda Tower. This and other exploits made him famous. Two other adelantados who kept journals of this voyage became important because Columbus's journal or log was lost. They were Dr. Diego Chanca, a physician from Seville and Michele de Cuneo, an old friend of Columbus. Also included on this second voyage were two military officers and six priests to convert the Indians. No member of the famous sea-faring Pinzon family who played such an important role in Columbus's first voyage sailed with him this time, but four of the famous Nino family were on board. A large crowd had gathered to watch the departure of this great fleet and it was a glorious sight as it made its way out to sea.

The docks at Cadiz and Seville were to remain busy for the next two centuries and even today Seville is one of Spain's leading ports. Amerigo and Bernardi were kept busy as were all outfitters of ships, but they rarely let anything interfere with the usual weekend dinners with Luisa, Pedro and Maria. Amerigo and Maria often found themselves on the dance floor of the gay Spanish cafes. Both were good dancers and both enjoyed each other's company. Maria, however, soon let it be known that another marriage for her would not be considered. The memory of her young husband who had died at sea just lingered on for her. As for Amerigo, he was kept too busy to think of marriage or much of anything else for Bernardi's health was failing and he had to take on more and more of the responsibility for the business.

Twelve of Columbus's fleet soon returned to Spain. They brought back news that Ojeda on an exploring expedition had found a gold mine on the island and in their cargo was gold worth 3500 double eagles. The ships, also, brought the sad news that none of the sailors left behind on Columbus's first voyage had survived. It seems that they had behaved outrageously. Instead of locating a good place for a permanent colony, as Columbus had instructed, they roamed the island in search of gold and women. Soon they so enraged Caonabo, the unfriendly Indian cacique, that he had them all hunted down and killed. The friendly cacique, Guacanagari, did his "timid best" according to historian, Samuel Eliot Morison, to save them but Caonabo was too much for him.

More news brought back told that Columbus had established a new settlement, which he named Isabella. He also had discovered twenty more large islands, but, no large and prosperous cities. On the islands he only found woodland inhabited with the same naked savages as on the first voyage. He named one of the islands Guadalupe for the Lady of Guadalupe, as he had promised. It still bears that name.

Bartholomew Columbus, Columbus's older brother, was in Paris when Columbus returned from his first voyage. He hurried to Spain and was received graciously by the King and Queen. They recognized him as a capable person and gave him command of three caravels to take supplies to Hispaniola. Bartholomew Columbus was to also play an important role in the early history of America, for he was a skilled cartographer and made many maps and he proved to be a more able leader than his two brothers. Meanwhile, Columbus unaware that Bartholomew was on his way, left his brother Diego in charge and hastily went in search of Cathay (China).

Leaving Diego in charge proved to be a mistake, for he was not a strong leader. He was at first too lenient and then too harsh. He is not to be blamed too much for his failure, for according to Oviedo in his History of the Indies, any governor to succeed in the Hispaniola of that time would have to be superhuman. Columbus according to his biographer, Morison, had already made serious mistakes. Beside leaving his weak but well-meaning brother in charge, he had given Ojeda a free hand in dealing with the Indians, and the choice of

Isabella for the site for his colony was a poor one. The harbor was poor and there was no close-by fresh water supply. The two hundred gentlemen proved also to be a disaster. When Columbus insisted that they pitch in and help to build the town, they were indignant. They grumbled, "We came to fight and to find gold not to do manual labor." Columbus refused to give them food unless they worked. This made them defiant and even more angry. Columbus was keenly disappointed when after exploring the interior to find that the island was not Cipangu (Japan). He was conscious of the unrest in the colony and realized the danger of mutiny, but he felt finding the mainland of Cathay would solve all the problems so he locked up all ammunition, and hurried across the Windward Passage to the land the natives called Cuba. They had told him that nearby Cuba was an island but he had high hopes that it would be the mainland of Asia. The little ships followed its southern coast of Cuba for seven hundred miles. "This cannot be an island," he thought, "It must be the southern coast of the Cathay, the province of Mangi." But again he had to admit he had found no rich cities, no richly clad merchants, no great buildings, or princely courts, only the same naked savages and they had no gold. Columbus then assembled all the crew made them sign a deposition declaring that Cuba must be part of a continent. He then turned southward to Jamaica.

For five months Columbus sailed from island to island without finding any sign of the great Cathay (China). His disappointment continued to be keen and he became ill. His officers hurriedly took him back to Hispaniola.

The conditions there were depressing. All food was having to be sent by caravel from Spain so regular voyages were being made and when each returned they brought back to Spain disillusioned settlers and many complaints. Many colonists on Hispaniola, too, fell ill with malaria or from drinking polluted water. Some suffered with bowel disorder possibly from eating strange fish. The only good news was of that Bartholomew had arrived with much needed supplies, and the discovery of the gold mine by Ojeda but the gold from that was hard to get and not plentiful.

Columbus had made careful plans, a canal to bring fresh water was being dug to connect with the nearest river and plans for a town had been laid out. It was to be like a miniature Cadiz. Around the town square two hundred huts were being built for temporary housing. Plans were also made for a church and a Governor's palace but the plans were never carried out.

Meanwhile to make matters worse, Ojeda and his garrison who had been commissioned to explore the island, took gold from the Indians and exhausted their food supply. Morison states that there was "hell in Hispaniola" when Bartholomew arrived. The conditions were hopeless.

So many complaints had reached Spain that the sovereigns sent a representative, Juan Aguado, to investigate the charges. Columbus now decided to return to Spain to talk directly to the sovereigns. This time he left Bartholomew in charge, with orders to find a more favorable capital site on the south side of the island and to abandon Isabella despite the work already done there. He, then, sailed for Spain on March 10, 1496.

Ojeda had subdued the Indians so they were no longer feared. He had captured the unfriendly cacique, Caonabo, by trickery. He invited him and his followers to make a state visit to Isabella. He insisted that they wear handcuffs and shackles, telling them that they were the fashionable jewelry of Spain and the trusting Indians allowed themselves to be handcuffed and shackled. The poor fellow and his followers were then thrown into jail and were among the Indians

Columbus took back to Spain with him on this return voyage. Columbus left only 650 colonists at Isabella. The rest had either died or had returned home.

Columbus, in his haste to return to Spain, took the shortest route, which proved to be disastrous. The winds were against him and it took twelve days to clear Hispaniola and it was two weeks more before he reached the island of Guadalupe. There they were greeted by Carib women armed with bow and arrows. These women were good bowman but no match for the Spaniards who quickly subdued them and forced them to give them much needed supplies. Legends sprang up about these women. They were claimed to be the Amazon women in the ancient legend. This according to Morison proved wrong. Their men were simply on the other side of the island hunting at the time.

After laying in supplies, Columbus continued his voyage on April 10, 1496, but because of contrary winds did not reach Cadiz until June 11, 1496. He had been away from Spain for two years and nine months.

Chapter XV

Columbus Returns from his Second Voyage and a Secret Voyage is Planned by the King

It was the year 1496. On June 11th of that year Columbus returned from his second voyage. He had explored many miles along the southern coast of Cuba and was sure it was the mainland of Asia, even though he had found nothing resembling the rich cities of the Indies that Marco Polo had described. As before he found only more naked savages and a small amount of gold. What had Columbus discovered? King Ferdinand was now more determined than ever to find out. He began plans for a secret voyage hoping to solve the puzzle.

The second homecoming of Columbus was not the joyous occasion of the first. There were no crowds waiting at the dock to greet him. Bernardi was dead but Amerigo and Vicente Yanez Pinzon were there. Pinzon was the captain of the Nina on Columbus's first voyage. They were distressed to see how much Columbus had aged. His hair had turned white and his formerly robust body was now gaunt. He was "plainly an ill and exhausted man." To further irritate him, his request for an audience with the sovereigns did not come until late in July. They were occupied arranging "prestigious marriages" for their children. While waiting for word from them, Columbus chose to reside with a humble priest instead of accepting two invitations to stay in castles.

He was dressed in the brown habit of a Franciscan monk when he came to the Bernardi place of business. "Why have I fallen so low?" he asked. "I must have been too proud. Now, I have put aside all my fine clothes and I'll dress like this the rest of my life," he added.

"You must not be so downcast," sympathized Vicente Yanez Pinzon. "You have a right to be proud."

"Yes," agreed Columbus "I have done all the things the king and queen asked of me. I have found a western route across the great Ocean Sea to the Indies. I have begun a trading post, and have brought back much gold."

"You have accomplished much and certainly you have much reason to be proud," added Amerigo.

"But 'pride goeth before a fall' sayeth the Bible and it must be true. Despite my good intentions, I have fallen! Why, Vicente, why?" asked Columbus sadly.

"There is no answer to your question, Columbus. Job, too, suffered without cause. Take consolation from his story. Remember that things turned out well for him in the end. I'm sure that you, too, will see better times," were the encouraging words of Pinzon to his distressed friend.

"I'm sure you have many interesting things to tell us," said Amerigo, hoping to get Columbus's mind on happier things.

"My return voyage was so long and so full of problems, all else is blotted out right now," confessed Columbus. "I was in such a hurry to get back to Spain that I took the most direct route across the water, as it turned out it may have been the shortest in distance but it was the longest in time. The winds were contrary and a great storm hindered us. I should have taken the same route as I took on my first voyage. On that voyage the winds blew northeast to the east all the way."

"Your supply ships followed that route," said Amerigo. "They reported favorable winds."

"Yes," said Columbus. "I instructed them to take the northeasterly route and they seemed to have made good time. I should have followed my own advice. Winds are very important for sailing vessels."

"It was the knowledge of the winds that made the early Greek and Roman voyages to the Indies easier," recalled Amerigo. "I remember reading in a translated old Roman manuscript about them."

"I thought early trade with the Indies was only possible across the great Arabian Desert." said the surprised Pinzon.

"No, Romans and Greeks could sail down the Red Sea to the Arabian Sea, then straight across to India." continued Amerigo, "They discovered that the wind on that part of the sea blew steadily southeast from May until October, and strangely enough the winds reversed direction from March to November for the return voyage."

"Why then, is that route no longer used?" asked Pinzon.

"Egypt was then a part of the great Roman Empire. Now it is under the control of the Muslim Turks. They charge excessive tariff so trade by that route is no longer profitable," explained Amerigo.

"A knowledge of the wind has always served sailors well," declared Columbus, "In Cordoba, there is a chapel called 'Our Lady of the Fair Winds'. Sailors go there to pray for fair winds."

"Winds are the horses of the sea, no doubt," agreed Pinzon.

Such conversation continued to be held during the time Columbus spent in Seville. In late July he was summoned to court in Valladolid. He again put together an impressive cavalcade. This time, however, he and his officers rode on mules instead of fine horses. The Indians, as before, were a prominent part of the cavalcade. They wore their feathered head dress and carried parrots. The featured Indian was the brother of the unfriendly Cacique, Caonabo, who had died before the ship reached Spain. His brother was speedily converted to Christianity, christened Don Diego and named chief of his tribe. In the parade he wore a golden necklace weighing many guineas and on his head was placed Caonabo's golden crown. Servants walked or followed in wagons carrying more brightly colored birds. The parade was viewed with the same delight and wonder as the first one.

Columbus was again graciously received by King Ferdinand and the Queen. He presented them with a clutch of gold nuggets as large as pigeon eggs and put in a plea for a fleet of five caravels, three to carry supplies to Hispaniola, and two for more exploration.

The sovereigns acceded to his request. They were disappointed that he had not found the golden cities but they realized that whatever Columbus had found, he had opened up the Ocean Sea to sailing vessels. They also had heard rumors that, in Portugal, a great fleet was being prepared for a voyage around Africa and they did not want Portugal to be the first to find a water route to the Indies.

Portugal was far ahead of Spain in ocean travel. Prince Henry, the Navigator, had gradually paved the way for voyages around Africa. On every voyage he encouraged the captain to dare to go farther southward and for every league he gave a special reward. In 1434, Gil Eannes, a Portuguese captain, under Henry's sponsorship, sailed to Cape Nun (Cape Nao) below the western bulge of Africa almost as far south as the equator. He set to rest the long held superstition that the waters near the equator were boiling. He also proved that ships could sail back against the prevailing northeasterlies. This old punning verse no longer was quoted:

> When old Cape Nun heaves into sight,
> Turn back, me lad, or else "Good night".

Gradually the western ports of Africa were opened up, the Gold and Ivory Coast, and then Malaqueta. In Malaqueta, a variety of pepper was found that was almost as hot as that found in the Indies.

In 1488, Bartholomew Diaz, another Portuguese, was the first to round the cape at the southern tip of Africa. He named it Cape Tormentos because of the dangerous waters. King John ordered that the name be changed to a more pleasant one, The Cape of Good Hope for obvious reasons. Bartholomew Diaz's voyage opened up a water way around Africa to India.

Little Portugal, after Prince Henry, continued to forge ahead of Spain in trade and sea travel and now the Spanish sovereigns were anxious to catch up. Columbus's ability as a seaman was appreciated so in spite of his two unfruitful voyage and the damaging reports from

Hispaniola they retained him as its governor and he was granted permission for a third voyage. King Ferdinand and Bishop Fonseca, however, continued with their plans for a secret voyage. They wanted more exploration by one who knew cosmography. Bishop Fonseca admired Amerigo's knowledge and unknowing to Amerigo at that time had planned to ask him to go on the secret voyage.

Although the sovereigns gave Columbus permission for the third voyage, they were slow in providing the money for outfitting the ships. Three hundred colonists were to be recruited to go to Hispaniola and that presented problems. Few volunteered for they had heard much unfavorable news. Finally the sovereigns offered a free pardon to those in jail who would go. Later, this rough element would add to Columbus's "already troubled colony".

Columbus returned to Seville after his visit to the Royal Court with much of his old vigor and enthusiasm. He was hoping to get the ship outfitted right away but no sailor would volunteer unless he was paid in advance and the sovereigns sent no money.

It was during this time of waiting that other interesting conversations took place in Bernardi's business house between Columbus, Amerigo, and other sea-faring men. Often, Juan de la Cosa and Vicente Yanez Pinzon were there and sometimes Bishop Fonseca. Pinzon had captained the Nina on Columbus's first voyage and Juan de la Cosa was recognized as an able navigator and map maker. He had been on Columbus's first and second voyage. They were actively seeking to persuade Columbus and the sovereigns to open the Ocean Sea to all ships.

Pinzon, whose family had figured so prominently in the first voyage was particularly anxious, "Columbus, there is so much that needs to be explored. You cannot hope to do it alone," pleaded

Pinzon. "You need to let others help you."

"I have a contract with the sovereigns and it must be followed. All exploration must be done according to that contract," stated Columbus. "I would be sailing today if the money was available."

"The area seems so vast. You have covered many leagues but still have found no signs of the rich cities or the rich spices that you are seeking. Wouldn't it be to your advantage to have more ships searching for them?" suggested Amerigo.

"You are tying the hands of the sovereigns. They want to keep their part of the bargain but also they must put first the interest of Spain," stated Bishop Fonseca. "It is not in Spain's best interest to allow you to keep a monopoly."

"You must listen to reason, Columbus," Juan de la Cosa said kindly. "It has been more than four years since your first voyage but still we are not sure what you have discovered."

"I have discovered a westward route to the Indies," Columbus stated bluntly. "And I am determined to be the first to find the rich cities. All I need are ships and time. I have already reached the mainland of Asia. Juan de la Cosa can vouch for that."

All eyes turned toward La Cosa. He had been with the second voyage and had, along with the rest of the crew, been forced to sign a deposition declaring Cuba to be the mainland of Asia.

La Cosa who was now skeptical of Columbus's claim stammered, "We sailed for many leagues along the coast of Cuba. It would have to be a very large island if it is not a continent."

"But didn't the Indians insist that it was an island?" asked Fonseca.

"Yes, but I am positive that it is the mainland of Asia," said Columbus.

"Maybe you should try to find Ptolemy's Strait of Catigara, which is supposed to be farther to the South," again suggested Amerigo. "It may be that your estimate of the width of the Asian continent is wrong. Toscanelli estimated it to be many miles less."

"I am sure that I have figured correctly," stated Columbus flatly.

"But search farther to the south on your next voyage," pleaded Amerigo. "Toscanelli estimated the distance to the island of Cipangu to be much farther than you. You believe it to be only 2600 Roman miles (2400 English miles). Your estimate may be a bit short," Amerigo ventured to suggest.

"Again, I am sure I am right," Columbus again stated emphatically.

Since the actual distance from Europe to Asia proved to be more like 10,600 (English) miles, Columbus, Toscanelli, and Ptolemy all figured short of the actual distance. It was not long after this conversation that Amerigo was approached by Bishop Fonseca and asked to go on a voyage of exploration as an observer. Fonseca was accompanied by the three Guerra brothers. They were wealthy merchants and ship builders in nearby Triana. They were, also, the chief bakers of bizcocho, or ship biscuits, often known as "hard tack", and that profitable business accounted for the greater part of their wealth.

"King Ferdinand is very anxious to find out if Cuba is a part of the mainland of Asia. He is making plans for a secret voyage. Since you seem knowledgeable on the subject of geography, he has instructed me to ask you to go as an advisor on this secret voyage. Will you go?" asked Fonseca.

"But," stammered Amerigo, "I am no sailor. Surely others are much more qualified than I."

"Perhaps there are others," agreed Fonseca, "but they are not in Spain. We must undertake this voyage immediately. It is in the interest of Spain. Many now, seem to be doubting whether Columbus has reached the Orient. What do you think?"

"From what I know, I, too, doubt whether Cipangu or Cathay have been reached, but the agreement! Columbus is my friend!" finished Amerigo.

"You will be a better friend if you are able to identify the land he has discovered," said Fonseca, "and as you know Columbus refuses to listen to reason."

"But Bernardi contracted to outfit three ships more ships for Columbus. I must abide by our contract." Amerigo protested.

"That," said Fonseca, "is why I have brought along the Guerra brothers. They realize that it is in the interest, not only of Spain, but of the entire shipping business to find out the truth as quickly as possible."

Anton Guerra, the eldest of the three brothers stepped forward. "We will finance and outfit Columbus's three ships if you will go. It is vital to our business that we find out the truth about these discoveries."

"Other merchants are joining us in encouraging this secret voyage," said the second brother.

"I am overwhelmed," said Amerigo, still amazed at the request. "I must have time to consider it."

"Take some time, but the ships are now being readied," said Fonseca. "And the sooner the better, this voyage will be very important for Spain and also for Columbus, and it must be kept secret."

Chapter XVI

Amerigo's First Voyage

It was the year 1497. Five years had passed since the great discovery and Columbus had made a second voyage. He had discovered twenty large islands and had founded the first Spanish settlement in the New World. He named it Isabella for the queen. It was located on the large island that Columbus believed to be Cipangu (Japan), but after exploring it far into its interior he had to admit he was wrong. It was not Cipangu. He then called the island Hispaniola, or Little Spain, the name it bears today and the two countries, Haiti and the Dominican Republic, now occupy it.

"What has Columbus discovered?" people wondered. Was it the Orient, as Columbus continued to claim? If so, where were those rich cities, the spices, and the fabulous silks? The meager returns from the first two voyages of Columbus had disappointed the sovereigns. The long war to drive the Moors out of the Spain had depleted the Spanish Treasury and they had expected lavish profits from what was thought to be a short water route to the Indies. The small amount of gold brought back by Columbus was scarcely enough to cover the expenses of the voyages. The cost of the new settlement, Isabella, was mounting, and it was not bringing in revenue. The great commercial firms that had financed many of the seventeen ships for the second voyage were pressuring the crown to open up the Great Ocean Sea to all ships. Yanez Pinzon and the other pilots who had been with Columbus on his first voyage were still urging Ferdinand to allow them to take part in the exploration. "It is not fair to us. We shared the risks of the first voyage." It was also rumored to the sovereigns that Columbus had suffered a nervous breakdown during his second voyage.

King Ferdinand and Queen Isabella had made solemn promises to Columbus and were reluctant to break them. When the news that the island was not Cipangu reached the palace, it seemed time though to review their decision. Isabella still wanted to give him more time but Ferdinand was a realist. "This new land," he reasoned, "covers too much area to leave to one man." Without consulting the queen he began making plans for a secret voyage to determine whether Cuba was the mainland of Asia, as Columbus claimed, or whether it was just a large island, as the native people insisted.

It was not too long after this decision that Fonseca and the Guerra brothers had come to Amerigo's office to ask him to go on the secret voyage. After they took their leave, Amerigo sat pondering at his desk. He remembered what he had written in his copybook when a student at the Monastery School:

> A Florentine who is not a merchant, who has
> not traveled through the world, seeing foreign
> nations and peoples, and then returned to
> Florence with some fortune, is a man who enjoys
> no esteem whatsoever.

Amerigo had often thought of going to sea and taking part in the great adventure. Now a way had opened for him. "I shall go," he had decided quickly. Preparation for the voyage was underway, but the final date for their departure was not set.

Amerigo, who had been named executor of Bernardi's will, had completed the settlement of the necessary affairs for Luisa and now felt free to go on the secret voyage. He had kept the news of the voyage secret even from these friends, Maria, Luisa and Pedro. Now, he knew, they must be told. "I will tell them tonight," he decided.

That night the conversation as it often did, turned to a discussion about Columbus's discovery. "Do you believe that Columbus has really reached Asia, Amerigo?" questioned Pedro.

"I honestly don't know. He, after exploring the large island he thought was Cipangu, has admitted that it is not Cipangu. All he found was more forests, and more of native inhabitants that he calls Indians. He still insists that the land just beyond is Cathay (China). On his second voyage he sailed along about seven hundred miles of the shore of the land the Indians call Cuba. He insists that it is the mainland of Cathay, but again found only more naked savages.

Luisa asked, "Have you heard that a secret voyage may be sent out, Amerigo? I have heard a rumor that Ferdinand is planning such a voyage."

"Yes, that is true, and he is delaying Columbus's third voyage until this secret voyage can be made. He feels that Columbus is no longer able to make a rational judgment. Ferdinand has been under great pressure to obtain more reliable information about the discovered land from the merchants and bankers who have largely financed the voyages of Columbus."

"But, are your sure?" asked Pedro.

"I know," Amerigo stated smiling, "because I have been asked to go along as an observer."

"You!" the surprised three exclaimed.

"But you must keep the voyage secret. Even the Queen is not to be told. She still hesitates because of the Royal promise to Columbus. Ferdinand, however, believes he has given Columbus enough time."

"But, why you? Surely there are many seamen more widely experienced than you," queried Maria with alarm.

"I can answer that question, Maria. It is because Amerigo knows more about geography. He is a good choice," stated Pedro.

"But is it fair to Columbus?" wondered Luisa. "What would Father say? He was such a good friend of Columbus, and you are, too, Amerigo."

"Your father and I often talked about the problem. Bernardi realized that it was of utmost importance to all commercial interests and to Spain. He believed that finding out what has been discovered was in Columbus's best interests, too."

"But do you believe that the voyage can be kept secret?" wondered Luisa.

"So far it seems to be a secret well-kept. Bishop Fonseca, the Guerra brothers, and the two main pilots are the only people, so far, that have been told, besides me and now you all, and of course, the pilots, Vicente Yanez Pinzon and Juan de las Cosa. One will be in command of the voyage and as you know both sailed with Columbus on his first voyage. Pinzon chose not to go on the second voyage, but now he is one of the chief pilots urging the King to open up the ocean for all ships. La Cosa, because of the map he is making wants to go so that the maps he is now drafting will be as accurate as possible. He doubts that Cuba is the mainland."

"It is logical that you would be asked to go on this secret venture, Amerigo," stated Pedro. "Your knowledge of geography and astronomy is no secret. But when will this momentous voyage begin?"

"The exact date has not been set, but it will be soon," declared Amerigo.

Later that evening as he walked Maria home, both were unusually quiet. "Secret or not, Amerigo, all ocean voyages are dangerous, as I well know. Remember what happened to the last four ships you sent out. They ran into a great storm, and although they were able to make it back to Cadiz, many lives were lost. Don't go, Amerigo!" pleaded Maria.

"But Maria, making an ocean voyage has been my dream since I first learned of Ptolemy's challenge. I was only a young man, then. Now, I have the opportunity," finished Amerigo.

"But what on earth is Ptolemy's challenge? He must have lived hundreds of years ago?" exclaimed Maria.

"Yes, that is true, but still no one has accepted his challenge. He challenged future men to find a more accurate way to determine longitude at sea. I want to be that man," stated Amerigo firmly.

Again both were unusually quiet. They sat side by side on Maria's patio for some time, then Amerigo put his arm around her shoulders. "Maria, you have become very dear to me," he confessed. "Often as I lay awake at night, I wonder if I could be so bold as to ask you to marry me."

Maria did not resist his embrace but snuggled closer to him. "You, also, Amerigo, have become more than just a friend to me," confessed Maria.

Amerigo's other arm completed the embrace and their lips met. " I love you," Amerigo murmured. Maria's arms tightened about him. They let go all the pent-up feelings that had been growing during the last five years.

"Will you marry me now?" Amerigo asked softly.

Maria slowly withdrew from his embrace and looked into the distance, remembering. "I have lost one husband to the sea," she said soberly. "I could not bear that agony again."

"But, Maria, I need you," begged Amerigo. "You have stirred within me feelings that I never thought I would have again."

"You, too, have known the loss of a loved one? I never knew," wondered Maria.

"It has been a sacred memory for me," confessed Amerigo. "It happened so long ago. I was only sixteen. The only other person that I have spoken to about this was my dear Uncle Giorgio, but now, I want you to know." Amerigo quietly related all about Elena, and their daughter.

"You must have loved her very much," Maria commented. "Do you know where she is today?"

"She died a short time before I came to Seville. My daughter, our daughter, came to Florence to tell me of her mother's death. With her, she brought a little three-year old girl. 'This is your granddaughter,' she said," Amerigo continued.

"I begged her to come with me to Seville, but she, like her mother, said she was a gypsy, and had a good life with a good gypsy husband, and would not."

Maria again sat quietly for some time, then she turned to Amerigo, "So you, too, have known what it is to love deeply, just as I loved Juan."

"Yes, Maria, I know, and I never expected to love again with the same passion, but I do now. I feel the same ecstasy with you in my arms. Marry me now, Maria. I need you," he pleaded.

"And I, too, feel about you as I did about Juan and again, I want to feel the closeness that exists only between a woman and her husband. I want to come first with someone again. Yes, I will marry you, Amerigo, but not until you return from this voyage."

Again they embraced and Amerigo said joyfully, "I love you, Maria. I love you very much. Please marry me, now, before we sail."

Maria again withdrew from his embrace. "I would beg of you not to go, but I know better than to try to persuade you. When the sea beckons a man, he cannot or will not refuse. I will marry you, but not until you return. I do not want to be widowed a second time."

With that Amerigo had to be satisfied. He walked home with an exhilarating lightness in his footsteps for he felt that a void in his life had been filled.

Within a few days, the three ships bound on this secret voyage slipped one by one down the Guadalquiver River to Cadiz, and thence to the open sea. Since it was a secret voyage, no record was kept of it, and many historians have doubted whether this voyage was ever made. Many others insist that it was. John Fiske, an American historian, Harry Harisse, who did much work on these early explorers, and Robert Levillier, an Argentine historian, are among the many that believe that it was made. They give as proof two maps, one made by Juan de la Cosa in 1500, and the famous Cantino Mappemonde of 1502. Both maps show Cuba as an island, and both show what seems to be the peninsula of Florida, which was not supposed to be discovered until 1513. Samuel Eliot Morison and others admit that secret voyages were made and that one must have come as far north as Florida.

The Cantino Map is an accurate and a beautiful one and it had to be made by made by a skilled cartographer. Some believed it was made by Bartholomew Columbus, who was a master of the art, but in his map dated 1503, Cuba is still shown as a peninsula jutting out from the mainland of Asia, and the tip of Florida is not shown so the Cantino map could not have been made by him. Another voyage must have been made.

Where did Amerigo go on this secret voyage? Why do these two maps, both of which are in existence today, prove that he made this voyage? According to careful study of commercial files, it began on May 10, 1497, and ended seventeen months later on October 15, 1498. Vicente Yanez Pinzon was in command. Juan de la Cosa and Ledecma were pilots. Amerigo went as an observer and as a cosmographer.

The landfall was the northern coast of Honduras. It passed west of Cuba, and proved that indeed it was an island. These three ships, as recorded in Amerigo's letter to his friend Soderini, then sailed to the north along the Yucatan, across the Gulf of Mexico. It may have touched the coast of Alabama at the mouth of the Apalachicola River. This point was named the End of April for the time of year that it was reached. While cruising along the coast the ships often stopped to explore the land and visit the inhabitants. The fleet skirted the coast of Florida, and, in June of 1498, possibly entered the large Tampa Bay and continued around the tip of Florida. Some believe that the voyage followed the coast north to the Chesapeake Bay. Then it turned east, and returned to Spain via the northern route by what is now the island of Bermuda and the Azores. Amerigo and the pilots had listened to Columbus, and knew the winds along this route would be favorable. They also sailed the northern routes to avoid the deadly calms of the "horse latitudes."

This voyage proved that Cuba was an island, and that although many thousands of miles of coastline had been skirted, they saw no sign of the rich cities of the Orient. "It could be Asia," Amerigo reported, "for I know that Asia is a vast continent." He also reported that he found no gold or anything that would bring immediate profit to the merchants. Amerigo wrote interesting accounts about animals and plants that he observed. He visited with these natives for twenty-seven days and reported details of their daily life for Europeans. He describes an aquatic village, with homes build on stilts. He visited a land called Lariab in the Yucatan. He described in detail the iguana lizard that the natives used as food. He said they were like small dragons without wings. The iguanas are even today used as food in tropical America.

Probably this voyage to the coast of North America was not followed up because Vasco da Gama's return from the Indies via the route around Africa happened about the same time as its return. Amerigo's voyage seemed unimportant and was soon forgotten in the frantic search for a southern strait that would lead into the Gulf of the Indies. Interest in lands to the west faded, and was revived only upon the discovery of the Pacific Ocean by Balboa in 1513, and by Ponce de Leon's discovery of Florida in the same year. Interest was particularly heightened in 1519, when Cortez found great quantities of gold in Mexico.

To return to the two maps that give evidence that this voyage was made, a copy of the Juan de la Cosa map dated 1500 can be seen today in the Lenox Collection in the New York City Museum. The Cantino Mappemonde dated 1502, is today on display in the famous Biblioteca Estense in Modena, Italy. The Cantino Map has a very interesting history. It seems that the Duke of Ferrara, Ercole d'Este, a typical Renaissance prince, was eager for knowledge about the new discoveries. Both King Emanuel of Portugal and King Ferdinand of Spain were very reluctant to give out any information as to the routes traveled by their ships. Ercole was curious. He sent a secret agent, Alberto Cantino, to Portugal with a double purpose. The first was to purchase Arabian horses for the Duke's stables and the second was to find out all he could about the new discoveries.

No doubt Cantino's ability as a horse trader made him shrewd enough to persuade a cartographer, name unknown, to design and draft a map from the information he had picked up on the waterfront. This cartographer was a skilled one, for this map is described as a "magnificent colored map" and very accurate. It also is the oldest except for La Cosa's to show the new America. The date of the map is also certain. It shows Cuba as an island and the tip of Florida. This information at that time could have come only from the Amerigo,

Pinzon, and La Cosa voyage of 1497-98. The map with a letter dated 19 November, 1502, was received by Ercole at Ferrara in Italy. Both the letter and the map are still extant.

This accurate and beautiful Cantino map was displayed in the ducal palace at Modena except for a brief period. It is said to have been thrown out of the window during one of the popular riots in Italy. A butcher picked it up and used it as a screen in his butcher's shop. It was soon rescued and "restored to all its pristine glory".

This Cantino map according to Samuel Eliot Morison "has driven historians and geographers almost frantic because of the continental area jutting out from its western border." What, they wonder, does it represent? Anyone's guess would be Florida, but history records that Florida was not discovered by Europeans until 1513. Morison then admits that secret voyages were made, but still refuses to give Amerigo credit.

If Amerigo made this voyage he would have been the first European to explore the southern coast of North America. Many believe that he falsely claimed to have made this voyage so he could claim to be the first to reach the mainland of the Americas. It is interesting to note that the name America was put on Waldsemuller's map, not because Amerigo reached the mainland first but because he was the first to recognize the land as a new continent and not part of Asia. At that time it was generally believed that Columbus had found a water route to the Indies even though he had failed to find any of its riches. Amerigo's discovery of a new continent was of enormous interest in Europe and his writings were widely read. He became very well known and Columbus was almost forgotten.

Chapter XVII

Amerigo's Marriage and Plans for a Second Voyage

Florence, 1498

To my long silent nephew, Amerigo Vespucci:

This has been a sad and strange year for Florence, and it makes me ashamed that such happenings could occur in our dear city. I will in this letter inform you of the unfortunate events that have transpired here, but first I must inquire about your health and ask if you now are a married man. You told me about your engagement to Maria in your last letter. It was a puzzling letter and gave no details as to your plans. I hope all has turned out as you hoped and that you and Maria will have a long and happy life together. I have missed having the love and comfort of a wife and have missed having children of my own. You and your brothers have been like sons to me and for that I am thankful.

But now I must relate the events that have taken place in Florence during the last year. As you remember, Florence was a chastened city after Lorenzo died and Savonarola took charge. He sincerely believed that God was speaking through him and quickly made sweeping laws and rules of reform that confused and confounded the people of Florence. He even defied the Pope just as he had defied Lorenzo. Pope Alexander invited him to visit him in Rome to make reform plans. Savonarola refused to go. The Pope, not handicapped, as Lorenzo was by a debilitating illness, took action. He excommunicated Savonarola and ordered Florence to get rid of him.

The people, too, by that time had enough of Savonarola's strict rule and demanded his departure from the city. Savonarola refused the command of the Signoria to go. A new gonfaloniere was chosen and I am both sorry and proud to say that it was our own Guido Antonio Vespucci who was chosen. He was the only member of the Signoria strong enough to take action. Savonarola was arrested. His few remaining followers marched to the Piazza in protest. Two agreed as in older days to prove that Savonarola was following God's will by walking barefoot over red-hot coals. Crowds stood anxiously by, some eager to see the event, others were frightened but mesmerized, stayed gazing in wonder. A fire was built and hot coals provided but just as the event was about to take place a great dark cloud appeared in the heavens and rain poured forth extinguishing the hot coals. No doubt, it was our Lord's way of expressing his disapproval of such a circus.

Soon Savonarola was charged with heresy and he confessed, no doubt after much coercion. He and one of his followers were hanged in the Piazza del Signoria. It was a sad day for Florence and for the Holy Church. He preached against the luxury, the greed, the extortion, and the intolerance that were corrupting Florence and indeed the whole church but he then became intolerant for he could not seem to understand or follow what Aristotle meant by the golden mean. It is sad for he was a powerful mover of men and with wisdom, he possibly could have made the reforms long overdue both in the church and in Florence.

By the way, recently there has been a lecturer in the University at Bologna who is advocating many of the same reforms as Savonarola but in a more subtle way. No doubt we will hear more of him later. He is from the Netherlands and is growing in prominence. He is Erasmus.

Now back to Florence, Guido is holding the people of Florence together with a firm hand but he is anxious for a less controversial figure to take his place. Again, your friend, Piero Soderini, is being considered. I will continue to keep you informed.

Now I have family news for you. All are well and Giovanni, Antonio's third son has at last got his fathers permission to come to Seville to be with you. I am sure you have missed your family and will welcome him but let us hear as soon as possible if you think his coming is the best for him and you. I know you have long wanted him and he has clung to the idea ever since you left for Seville.

With high regards for you, Amerigo, and with hopes of hearing from you soon, I remain,

Your affectionate uncle,

Giorgio Antonio.

September, 1498

To my most beloved and respected uncle, Giorgio Antonio,

I am now somewhere on the great Ocean Sea and almost I, hope, to the end of a long voyage for the King of Spain. By my reckoning we are north of the Azores islands.

The purpose of this voyage was to determine if Columbus has reached Asia as he believes he has. Since King Ferdinand and Queen Isabella had made an agreement not to allow any ships to sail to the new lands without Columbus's permission, this voyage had to be kept secret. That is why I could not inform you of it before I left.

On this voyage we have passed many islands and sailed along many leagues of coast. The extent of the coast is so vast that it could be Asia --- but never did we find any clue of the rich cities of Cathay, or any of the spices of the Indies. We saw only many naked savages, such as the ones Columbus brought back after his first voyage. We also saw great forests and many species of birds and animals. The people, the birds, and the animals are different from those in Europe, also different from those we have seen or heard about in Africa, and certainly not like the ones I've read about in the Orient. What Columbus has discovered is a still big puzzle and I hope I can help put the pieces of the puzzle together.

Columbus, as I have written you, is certain that he has reached the mainland of Asia. On our voyage we have determined that the land that he claimed to be mainland of Asia is a very long island, many leagues long, but not very wide. We sailed completely around it and it is definitely an island and not the mainland.

On our voyage over, we followed closely the same sea route that Columbus had followed and returned by much the same route that he did. We were lucky that no storms hindered us. What Columbus did when he was the first to venture across the Great Ocean Sea is a great feat and he has discovered much land but what that land is, remains a big question.

But now as our ship gets closer to Spain, my thinking is on other things. I wrote you briefly before I sailed telling you that lovely Maria had consented to marry me. She insisted on waiting until I returned from this voyage. That was now almost a year and a half ago. Will she still be of the same mind? I am as anxious as a young man with his first love. I will soon know, and you will be one of the first to share my joy or my doom.

Your nephew,

Amerigo Vespucci

P.S.   Your letter was waiting for me when I arrived in Seville. I will welcome Giovanni and I promise to try to be as good an uncle to him as you have been to me. And more good news, Maria and I plan to be married soon. I am thankful and happy.

It was the year 1498. Amerigo returned from his first voyage on October 15. This was the voyage that has caused so much controversy for it was never recorded. It was ordered by King Ferdinand and kept secret even from the Queen because she still wanted to give Columbus more time.

As Amerigo's ship sailed up the Guadalquiver River to Seville, he was on deck eagerly scanning the shore. He had been gone for almost seventeen months. Would Maria still consent to marry him or had she changed her mind after his long absence? His heart leaped up when he saw three people walking along the river banks. They were waving at the ship.

Could it be Maria, Luisa and Pedro? He hardly dared hope. As the ship passed the Torre del Oro, it seemed to give him a warmer welcome than the one on his arrival about seven years ago. He felt like he was coming home, for now Seville was seeming more like his home.

His eyes remained on the three waving figures. He discerned two women and one man. "Yes," he cried, "it is Maria, Luisa and Pedro," and he waved back vigorously.

When the ship docked, he was the first to disembark and happily Maria was soon folded into his arms. The other two stood back but soon they, too, greeted Amerigo warmly. It was the welcome that he had hoped for.

Also on hand to greet him was Bishop Fonseca, who said, "Come to my office as soon as you have rested up a bit for we are anxiously awaiting your report. Did you ever find the rich cities of the Orient?"

"No, I'm sorry to say," responded Amerigo, "but we sailed along many leagues of mainland that seemed vast enough to be Asia, but no rich cities, only naked savages as Columbus has found. We also ascertained that Columbus's Cuba is an island and not connected with the mainland."

"So it is certain that Cuba is not Cathay, but what is it? We will need more such voyages," said Fonseca.

"Yes," agreed Amerigo.

"And as to the use of the astrolabe. Did you find it useful?" Fonseca continued to ask eagerly.

"Yes, it is more accurate than just the compass alone," stated Amerigo.

"So far, this voyage has been kept secret. The Queen still does not know but now by her consent as well as that of the King, the restriction on other voyages has been lifted. Now anyone who desires may get permission to go," disclosed Fonseca.

"That is good," replied Amerigo, "for now I am certain that the extent of the area is too great for only one man to explore."

"No doubt many more voyages will be needed to determine what Columbus has discovered. I will expect you later for a full report," said Fonseca as he left the group.

Maria and Luisa had not been idle during the long months of Amerigo's voyage. Definite plans had been made for the wedding. The ceremony was soon performed in a small chapel of the great Cathedral, the one that opened out on the Court of Oranges, Amerigo's favorite place. They had a wedding breakfast at Cafe de las Sierpes, their favorite restaurant, and Amerigo moved over into Maria's home.

Her home was a pleasant villa built around a patio as are most Spanish homes. It had been left to Maria and her brother, Fernando, by their father. Fernando and his wife, Julia, lived in the west quarter.

It was a satisfactory arrangement for Amerigo, for outfitting ships for Columbus had not been profitable. Their quarters were pleasant to Amerigo for they opened up on an orange shaded patio. Several evenings later, they were sitting side by side on this patio. The moonlight was soft but bright enough for Amerigo to see Maria's lovely face as she smiled up at him. They sat there contentedly but finally Amerigo said, "I know now what my uncle Giorgio meant when he said no man's life is really complete without a loving wife. This must be what it is like in Paradise."

"To me," Maria whispered, "just having you back safely makes my life complete, but now tell me about that strange, far away land over the Great Sea. It seems you told Bishop Fonseca that Paradise could be found there."

"It is beautiful with its great virgin forest as I imagine Paradise would be, but there is one thing lacking. In that great place there is no Eve and Paradise cannot be complete without Eve," his arm tightened around her and she snuggled closer to him, as he whispered, "My paradise will always be where you are."

"I hope you will remember that when Mistress Sea again beckons you," replied Maria coyly.

Amerigo looked up at the sky. Though the moon was bright, some stars were popping out. "There is so much that is unknown in that strange land. Ptolemy's Strait of Catigara has not been found. We still do not know what Columbus has discovered. Someone has to unlock its secrets, and I want to have a part of it," Amerigo confessed.

"I know," sighed Maria, "it must be my fate to love sea-faring men."

"How large is our world?" Amerigo continued to wonder. "How far is it to the real Cipangu? Toscanelli estimated possibly than 3000 leagues but Columbus figured much less. It may be farther than either of them imagined. 'The mystery of longitude,' Ptolemy said, 'must be solved before we know.' Yes, solving that problem is my dream. Yes, I probably will go to sea again but no matter where I am we can look up at the same moon and the same stars and we can feel close."

"But perhaps, not as close as I would like to be," whispered Maria.

"And not as close as I would like to be either," he answered as he took her into his arms.

Soon Bishop Fonseca returned from Cordoba after reporting to the king there. He brought a message from Ferdinand asking Amerigo to come immediately to the Royal Court to report directly to him.

"It is an honor," said Maria when she was told, "but we are just wed. Must we be separated so soon? Do you have to go now?"

"Yes Maria, but not without you. You shall accompany me and what about asking Luisa and Pedro to come along?" suggested Amerigo.

"That sounds nice," agreed Maria.

"And afterward, perhaps we can take that pilgrimage to visit the Lady of Guadalupe. I remember that you hoped to go there some day. This will be our chance."

"I will like that," she answered as she thought, "Life with Amerigo will never be dull."

In a few days the four set out on horseback for Cordoba and the court of the King and Queen. The Royal Court, as the one in France, often moved about in those days but most often it was held in Cordoba or Valladolid. The distance to Cordoba was not too great so it was a pleasant holiday. They set out on horseback with grooms carrying their luggage in wagons.

At court, they were received graciously and assigned rooms in a wing of the palace, the Alcazar in Cordoba. Amerigo was soon summoned to appear before King Ferdinand who listened attentively to a full report of the secret voyage. "As Bishop Fonseca said, 'You have brought back more questions than answers.' We need to know more about this great expanse of land that Columbus has discovered," said Ferdinand. "Your knowledge of geography can be very useful. Will you go on another voyage, Amerigo?" he asked.

"Yes," was Amerigo's answer, "for I want to search for Ptolemy's Strait of Catigara. He believed it to be many leagues south of the equator. He believed it would connect the Ocean Sea with the great gulfs of the Indies."

"Then another voyage must be planned without delay," insisted the king.
"Bishop Fonseca will inform you."

"I will await your call," said Amerigo, as he bowed and took his leave.

Meanwhile Maria, Luisa, and Pedro were resting in their rooms, "I never expected to sleep in a palace," giggled Luisa, as delighted as a school girl. "How very fine it is. Look at the tapestries and even the covering on the wall is fine damask."

"It is beautiful. We can pretend we are queens for a night," agreed Maria. "If these palaces have so many rooms, no one has ever tried to count them. I wonder if all are as lovely as this one."

"This would be something to tell our grandchildren about if we ever have any," said Maria, and then added after a pause, "I hope Amerigo and I can have a child, but we are not young."

The next morning they began the long trip north and west to the Estremadura, the most rugged and mountainous part of Spain. The Monastery that was the home of the famous virgin had been built there in the place where she had lay buried for those many years.

This part of the journey was slow and hard. They rode mules for the way was too steep for horses and they took very little baggage and left most in Cordoba with a groom.

All four were weary for this road was rocky as well as steep. Often they had to dismount and lead their mules. At last they reached the top of the mountain. They looked down and saw the monastery in the valley. It was such a beautiful sight that all four gasped in wonder.

"There it is," said Don Pedro, and they all gazed in silence and reverence. The monastery was nestled down in the most beautiful valley they had ever seen.

"Now I'm sure why this is the most lovely and sacred place in Spain. All who have visited here have said that the torturous journey was worth it and I agree," said Luisa finally.

"It has been one of my heart's desire," confessed Maria. "Thank you, Amerigo, for helping make another one of my dreams a reality. I have slept in a palace and now this."

"We still have a few miles to go," said practical Don Pedro dryly. "Let us get started."

"Yes," agreed Amerigo, "but it is downhill all the way."

The weary travelers slowly urged the sure-footed mules down the rocky slope. Sometimes the way was so steep they walked and led their mount cautiously, but finally they reached the gates of the monastery and rang the large bell.

An old monk opened it and welcomed them. He then showed them to the quarters reserved for pilgrims to the shrine. Soon he returned with refreshments and suggested, "It's late and you must be weary. Rest tonight and in the morning you can visit Our Lady."

"Thank you, we would like that," they all agreed.

"We are indeed weary," said Luisa.

The next morning after a restful night and a substantial breakfast, the old monk returned and ushered them into the sanctuary of the virgin. The hall was large and was lighted with beautiful chandeliers. The covering of the walls was of rich tapestries and they treaded on priceless oriental rugs. The atmosphere in the room was one of quiet reverence; no word was spoken as the four followed the measured footsteps of their guide. He led them to a little throne. On it sat the tiny virgin. A soft light was shining on her sweet face. Her garments were magnificent but it was the figure itself that held their reverent attention for her eyes seemed to be looking directly at the visitors. In her arms was a figure of the little baby Jesus. He was also clad in a magnificent garment.

The four had worshiped in many chapels and had bowed before many virgins but this tiny Lady of Guadalupe moved them to a deeper reverence than they had ever experienced before. They gazed in silence and then each lighted a candle and made their private prayer. A bell tolled, the old monk beckoned to them and they slowly followed him back to their quarters.

"Now," Amerigo said as they were again alone. "I can understand why Columbus made this long pilgrimage to give thanks to The Lady. She seems to have special power."

"She has saved Spain many times," said Maria to Amerigo. I begged her protecting spirit to go with you on your next voyage."

The next morning, much refreshed and renewed the four mounted their mules and began the long way back home. "We all will be better people because we have visited her," said Luisa, and all silently agreed. Very little conversation took place on the rough and rugged trip back to Cordoba. They were all wondering quietly about the Lady of Guadalupe. Her presence lingered.

A letter to Amerigo from his brother, Antonio Vespucci was awaiting him when they returned home. It announced the eminent arrival of Giovanni, Amerigo's favorite nephew.

"He will be here in time to accompany me on my next voyage,"

Amerigo stated happily. "My heart has hungered to see my family. I am overjoyed."

Amerigo along with Bishop Fonseca made careful plans for the next voyage. Alonso de la Ojeda would captain the fleet and Juan de la Cosa would be one of the pilots. Much time, however, was left to be with Maria. Their love had matured slowly but now their lives seemed filled with quiet contentment. Amerigo's eyes when he looked at Maria said, "I love you" and her eyes warmly responded.

Giovanni soon arrived and they with Luisa and Pedro took delight in showing him Seville. He showed boyish eagerness in all that he saw, "An underground stable that can hold two thousands horses!" shouted Giovanni in amazement. He seemed to be filling the need for the child they all four had yearned for.

Chapter XVIII

The Third Voyage of Columbus

It was not until May 1498, that Columbus was able to begin his third voyage, the voyage in which he touched the mainland for the first time. His first landfall was the large island of Trinidad with its three towering mountain peaks. He named it Trinidad for the three mountain peaks reminded him that he had put this voyage under the protection of the Holy Trinity. The island still bears that name.

From Trinidad, Columbus steered his three ships across the Gulf of Paria to a peninsula that he called Isla de Gracias. He landed there on August 5, 1498, and if Amerigo's 1497 voyage did not in fact take place, he was the first European to set foot on the mainland. At that time, however, Columbus thought it was another island.

Later Columbus, after noting the great quantity of fresh water pouring forth from the Orinoco River, thought it might be a continent but never proclaimed it. He decided that it could the Garden of Eden. He then sailed north and sighted the island that he named Margarita, for the baby princess born in Austria. Unfortunately for him, he did not land for this turned out to be the famous Pearl Coast that others found so profitable. On a nearby island, he encountered his brother Bartholomew and the two of them returned to the new settlement on Hispaniola. Isabella had been abandoned. Bartholomew's new settlement had a protected harbor and an abundant supply of fresh water. It was named Santo Domingo. Today this city is the capital of the Dominican Republic and still bears that name.

Despite the better location, the settlement only contained temporary thatched huts. Bartholomew had the same trouble that Columbus had. The Spanish hidalgo refused to do work that "would dirty their hands and the Indians were poor carpenters". The few colonist willing to work were often ill.

To complicate matters Francisco Roldan who had been appointed chief justice by Columbus led a revolt against Bartholomew, and the three supply ships that Columbus had sent by Carvajal had fallen into his hands. The crew of Carvajal's ships was largely made up of men just released from jail. They were easily persuaded by Roldan to join him.

Columbus and Bartholomew in order to bring peace to Santo Domingo restored Roldan to his former position and promised free passage home to all who wanted to go. A new system of distributing land called Repartimiento or Ecomientia was adopted. This system was later followed by most Spanish settlements in America. It allowed every Spaniard a considerable plot of land and made all Indians living on that land the personal slaves of the Spanish land owner. The Indians consented to this for it meant that they would no longer have to pay the gold tribute that had earlier been imposed upon them.

Roldan still was not satisfied. He seized one of Carvajal's ships and, getting together many discontented settlers, sailed for Spain.

There, they complained bitterly about Columbus and his brothers. It is true that they had proved to be poor administrators. According to Samuel Eliot Morison, they were "weak when they should have been firm, and ruthless at the wrong time, and had not saved the Indians from exploitation."

Columbus was to return two of his supply ships to Spain, and as he had very little gold or pearls to return, he filled the ship with Indians to be sold as slaves. One ship, it seems, included many young and pregnant girls. The queen was indignant and had them returned to Hispaniola.

The cost of supplies for the new colony kept mounting and no revenue was being realized and furthermore there seemed no hope of any. King Ferdinand and now even Queen Isabella decided that something must be done. They sent Francisco de Bobadilla who was a longtime trusted official of the crown to Hispaniola. He was given complete power to deal with the situation and Columbus was ordered "to obey him in all things."

When Bobadilla arrived seven bodies of Spaniards were dangling from the gibbet. Bartholomew and Columbus were in the interior of the island hunting down the remainder of the rebels. Diego, who had been left in charge, informed Bobadilla that five more Spaniards would be hanged the next day. Bobadilla presented his credentials to Diego, then promptly arrested him. When Columbus and Bartholomew returned, they, too, were arrested. Bobadilla had no trouble obtaining evidence against them and all three were put in chains and were sent to Spain on the next ship. When they were out to sea, the captain of the ship offered to remove their chains but Columbus refused, saying, "My sovereigns ordered me to submit to Bobadilla's orders. By his authority I wear these chains and I shall continue to wear them until they are removed by order of the sovereigns," and this

Columbus did. He kept them on till he was summoned to court six weeks later.

He, again, stayed in the monastery in Triana until Queen Isabella ordered that the chains be removed and sent him 10,000 ducats for his travel expense to court.

When Columbus arrived at court, he was kindly received by the sovereigns. They promised that Bobadilla would be recalled and that justice would be done in Hispaniola, but they did not offer to return Columbus to his colony. Instead, they offered him a villa, a pension, and a ducal title if he would give up his claim and settle down. Columbus flatly refused this offer.

Months passed. Bobadilla was recalled, and Don Nicolás de Ovando was appointed governor of the Island and the mainland of the Indies. Columbus was to retain his title as Viceroy and Admiral of the Ocean Sea and was also given permission to send an agent to Hispaniola to collect all the gold due him. His friend, Alonso de Carvajal, was again called upon to carry out this mission.

Ovando sailed from Cadiz on February, 1502, with a fleet of thirty ships and 2,500 sailors, soldiers, and new colonists. Columbus, because of this, at last realized that the sovereigns did not intend to return him to Hispaniola to govern the island so he then petitioned them for money and ships for a fourth voyage of discovery. They quickly granted him permission on condition that he not stop at Hispaniola. He immediately began making preparations for his fourth voyage.

Chapter XIX

Amerigo's Second Voyage

It was the year 1499. Amerigo was again on the high seas. King Ferdinand was serious about the need for more exploration and on May 18th, a fleet of four or five caravels under the leadership of the soldier, Alonso de Ojeda set out for the new land. Amerigo was in command of two or three of these caravels. They had been outfitted by the great Commercial Houses in Seville. This expedition had a dual purpose. Ojeda, the soldier, was to search the Caribbean for any signs of English ships. It had been rumored that they may have been encroaching on Spanish waters. The caravels under the command of Amerigo were to search for the strait that Ptolemy believed would connect the two large bays, the Sinus Magnus and the Sinus Gangeticus. It was through this strait that Chinese treasure was being carried from Cathy (China) to the Indies and then on to Europe. Amerigo was also to determine what of commercial value could be found in the newly-discovered land.

Alonso de Ojeda, the leader, was a colorful figure. He had accompanied Columbus on his second voyage. It was he and his men who had discovered the gold mine on Hispaniola had successfully subdued the Indian uprising. He was born in 1470, to a respectable family in Guernica, a town in Castile. As a young man he had been a squire of the powerful Duke of Medina and was a favorite of Bishop Fonseca. He had attracted the attention of Queen Isabella by daring to dance on the topmost ridge of the Giralda Tower in Seville.

This was Amerigo's second voyage and his nephew Giovanni was sailing with him. Vicente Yanez Pinzon who had been captain of the Nina on the first voyage of Columbus was believed to be the chief pilot for Amerigo's ships. Juan de la Cosa was the chief pilot for Ojeda. The fleet would keep together until they made landfall and then would separate to perform their separate missions.

Amerigo and young Giovanni were on deck shortly before the ships reached the Canary Islands. "We have been sailing south for several days. "Why," wondered young Giovanni, "do we have to sail this far south for supplies? The Indies are due west of Spain. Wouldn't we have saved time by picking up all our supplies in Cadiz and sailing straight west?"

"We are headed for the Canary Islands. It is true that they are about 500 miles south of Spain, but they are also many miles further to the west. We have been sailing southwest, and are many miles closer to our destination, and, if Ptolemy was right, we will find the Strait of Catigara, the strait for which we are searching south of the equator," answered Amerigo.

"Then I guess we haven't wasted time," replied Giovanni.

"No, and the supplies we are to pick up there are mostly live animals - chickens, pigs, and cattle. The animals will have a shorter voyage and that will ensure that we have fresh meat for a much longer time," explained Amerigo, and added, "We will replenish our supply of wood and water there also. Spain owns these islands."

"It makes sense now that I know we are farther to the west," said Giovanni. "It is fortunate that Spain owns these islands."

"Yes, and for many years they were known to the ancients as the Fortunate Islands. They are now becoming useful as stepping stones to the west," agreed Amerigo. "Columbus used them."

"Spain is certainly fortunate to have them now," said Giovanni. "Tell me about them."

"These islands have a long history. The Phoenicians may have been the first to discover them, probably before the time of Christ. The Romans also knew of them. Pliny, the Roman historian, is the one who referred to them as the Fortunate Islands," replied Amerigo.

And so began Giovanni's education. Amerigo would play the part of an Italian uncle to Giovanni, just as Giorgio Antonio did for him.

The ships were in the Canaries for several days picking up supplies. When they were again on the high sea Giovanni asked, "Why are they still not called the Fortunate Islands?"

"Many years had passed, and these islands were forgotten. When they were rediscovered, their discoverer did not know their history, "explained Amerigo.

"I did see many canary birds when we stopped there. Is that how they got their names?" Giovanni continued to question.

"No," smiled Amerigo. "They were named for the wild dogs or canines that were roaming the island then, and in time the many yellow birds there became known as canaries, too."

It was 7:30, and time for Giovanni to turn the half-hour glass. He had joined the crew on the ship ,as a cabin boy or "page of the broom" as they were often called. Each ship always signed on several cabin boys, and each was required to be on duty for eight hours. Each half-hour, they turned the half-hour glass or ampoletta. None of the clocks of that day because of the continual motion of the sea could keep accurate time on shipboard.

Amerigo had been up early watching the night sky and to be with his young nephew. He enjoyed hearing Giovanni's sweet soprano voice as he turned the half-hour glass for the last time during his watch and sang out the daytime ditty.

> Blessed be the light of day,
> And the Holy Cross we say,
> And the Lord of Veritie,
> And the Holy Trinity.
> Blessed be the immortal soul,
> And the Lord who keeps it whole,
> Blessed be the light of day,
> And He who sends the night away.

Sailors on all sailing vessels are usually a pious group. They knew the danger of sailing on the high seas, and believed firmly that a safe voyage was in the Lord's hand. It had long been a tradition for all on board to go just before sailing to the nearest church to celebrate mass. They also observed a semi-religious ritual every day on shipboard.

Morning and evening prayer was led by the ship's captain or by a priest if one were on board, and a semi-religious ditty was sung by the cabin boy, every half hour. It was sung by him because it was believed that God would be better pleased by the voice of an innocent.

The cabin boy after the Daybreak Ditty, recited or chanted the Pater Noster and the Ave Maria. He then adds: "God give us good days, good voyage, good passage to the ship, Sir Captain and Master, and good company. Amen." He finishes with "So let there be a good voyage, many good days, and may God grant you grace, Gentlemen of the Afterguard and Gentlemen of the Forward." The night watch then gives way to the morning watch.

The night watch had scrubbed the decks down with salt water that was hauled up in buckets, using stiff brooms made of twigs. When the new crew takes over, the next cabin boy sings this ditty:

> Good is that which passeth,
> Better that which cometh,
> Seven is past and eight floweth,
> More shall flow if God wills it.
> Count and pass make voyages fast.

After he turns the half-hour glass for the first time on his watch, he sings out:

> On deck, Mr. Mariner, of the right side
> On deck in good time, Mr. Pilot.
> Shake a leg.

And so the day begins. The mariners who are coming on duty grab a ship's biscuit, a garlic clove, a bit of cheese, and perhaps a pickled sardine, and shuffle off to the poop deck.

The helmsman then gives the course to the captain of the watch. The captain repeats it to the helmsman, who repeats it again. They want to be sure no mistake is made.

A lookout is posted aft and forward, and the off-going captain of the watch transfers his reckoning from the slate to the logbook. The cabin boy wipes the slate clean for the next captain. The caulkers and carpenters prime the pump, and if the ship has leaked water during the night, they pump it dry. So begins a new day as the off-duty watch eats breakfast and goes off to sleep.

The head captain's servant brings him a bucket of salt water for washing and a cup of fresh water for drinking. The servant then brings the captain's breakfast. After eating the captain comes on deck and looks around the horizon and sings out a pious "Gracias a Dios" for fair weather. He then chats with the Master or the pilot.

Each crew is responsible for the ship during their eight-hour watch. In case of a storm, however, all hands are summoned.

During each watch, the orders are given by the acting captain or the chief boatswain. He usually carries a pipe around his neck and plays on it a variety of signals. Orders on these small vessels were given orally. It is interesting that the orders are obeyed promptly. All know that obeying them often is a matter of life or death.

Toilet seats are hung over the rails, one forward and one aft. They were called jardines. Instead of "the often smiled at corncob" the sailors used a tarred rope that dangled into the water.

On shipboard, one hot meal was served a day, usually at noon and on deck if the weather permitted. The staff of life for seaman was the sea biscuit or hardtack as it is usually called. The Spanish word for them is bizcocho. The making of these was the main business of the Guerra brothers in Triana. They financed many voyages to the new land including Columbus's third voyage and they, themselves, later sailed on several voyages.

The hot meal of the day always had saltmeat or salted codfish and olive oil. Occasionally they had cheese, chick peas, or other lentils, and for a special treat they might be served honey, almonds, or raisins. The fare was so often repeated that it became monotonous but to many, at that time, it was a feast. Certainly it was to many cabin boys, for often they were runaway apprentices who were escaping from a stingy master.

On this second voyage of Amerigo, fair weather and favorable winds were recorded. After leaving the Canary Islands the fleet sailed west by south and sighted land in twenty-seven days. With favorable wind a sailing vessel can make a hundred miles a day. The average is usually eighty-five. Amerigo figured that they had sailed one thousand leagues (about 3000 miles) west of the Grand Canaries.

Land was sighted. The ships were now in the Torrid Zone and the North Star was only about six degrees above the horizon. It was Giovanni first sight of the new land and the natives without meaning to were putting on a show for him. Many were walking along the shore in their usual state of nudity. A small boat load of seamen rowed to shore with small bells, mirrors, and other trifles, hoping to trade with them but they were too shy and retreated to the woods. The seamen paddled back to the ships and since there was no good harbor in which to anchor overnight the entire fleet sailed along the coast searching for one.

After several days a suitable harbor was found. The natives there were also shy but they were intrigued by the tinkling bells and the mirrors. Soon they became friendly and a lively exchange of the bells for pearls took place. Amerigo wrote that they even gave them gold, demanding nothing in return. Gold seemed to be little prized by them. Their riches seemed the splendid colored feathers of the native birds. The Spaniards made signs that they needed food and as night was coming on we bade them farewell and returned to our ships.

The next morning Amerigo wrote, "We, again, took the boats and rowed ashore. When we reached shore the natives gave us a supply of fresh fruit and fish. The water in our barrels was low and stale so we filled them with the sweet fresh water. For that we were thankful."

The fleet split up at this point according to the plan; they were to remain together on the high seas, and then Ojeda with Juan de la Cosa as pilot would sail northward to the Caribbean, visit Margarita, the Island of Pearls that had been discovered by Columbus. They searched the waters for English ships for some time but found none. They visited Hispaniola before sailing back to Spain.

The other ships under Amerigo's command did not tarry long in that place. They were pleased and grateful for the warm reception by the Indians but were anxious to sail farther south.

As they sailed to the south, Amerigo noted that the days and nights were nearly equal. The land was flat and the sea often seemed higher than the land. The water became fresh far out to sea so they soon realized that they were sailing in the mouth of a great river. A great thunderstorm "blackened the sky" and lightning "caused blue flames to engulf the mast heads and yardarms." Because of this they named the large island in the mouth of the river the Island of Fire or St. Elmo's Fire.

After the storm Amerigo with twenty men sailed up this river for four days. The only sign of humans was the smoke from many fires. They saw no villages and found no suitable place to land their boat. The undergrowth was too thick along this great river. They called it the River of Concealed Fire (Rio de Taco Cecho). This name was the first given to Amazon according to the Ruijack map of 1508.

The twenty men took turns rowing and in all they traveled about seventy miles upstream. Often they attempted to land but were prevented by the tangle of roots and branches in the Brazilian jungle. Amerigo noted many water fowls and parrots of many colors. He heard the melodious song of birds. They called one branch of this great river the River of the Birds (Rio des Aves). The river flowed from west to the east and averaged about sixteen miles wide.

Since finding no place to land, they returned to the ship and sailed southward. They then entered a great estuary of the Amazon, known today as the Para River. They named it the Rio Grande.

While in the Delta of this large river, Amerigo realized that they had crossed the equator for the North Star dropped to the horizon. He, with Pinzon, the Navigator, and their crew were the first to cross the equator in the western hemisphere.

Amerigo and a crew sailed up this river for two days. They, again, found no landing place because of the tangle of roots and branches. This river was also very large. Amerigo estimated it to be about three leagues or twelve miles wide and it flowed from south to north.

After exploring the delta of these two rivers for a fortnight, they sailed southward following the coast of Brazil. Because of the enormous amount of water brought down by these two immense rivers, they were sure that they flowed from a great land mass and that no passage to the west could be found there. They sailed as fast as possible not stopping until they were about eight hundred miles south of the equator. Night after night, Amerigo studied the sky in the southern hemisphere. He hoped to find a celestial pole star. He did not find one but did observe four bright stars that seemed to be in a fixed position near the south pole. He described them to be in the shape of a mandolin. They are now called the Southern Cross.

On July the fourteenth, their progress was slowed by the pressure of the equatorial current. The current that had been about sixteen miles an hour now increased to forty and sometimes up to eighty miles and hour. They were on the farthest east point of Brazil. Amerigo attempted to avoid the swift current by sailing straight out to sea but the strong ocean current was too much for them, and they could not escape it. They gave up and sailed with the current from the southeast to the northwest. Amerigo was the first to call attention to the equatorial currents. He was disappointed for he had hoped to find Ptolemy's Strait of Catigara farther to the south.

The ships pushed by the ocean current sailed north to the Island of Trinidad, the island of Columbus's land fall on his third voyage. Here the Indians were friendly and they got food, water, and some pearls. These natives, Amerigo described as a kind people. They did not tarry long here but again sailed this time to the west.

The Indians on the next stop were not so friendly. They came with bows and arrows and a severe fight took place. The superior weapons of the Spaniards soon routed the Indians but the crew was weary and some seriously wounded. The ship remained anchored in this harbor for twenty days so the crew could rest up and so the doctor could take care of the wounded.

During these twenty days and nights Amerigo studied the heavens. He was hoping to find a way to determine longitude. He brought "a fresh mind" to the problem and was one of the first men to use a scientific method. He studied the night sky and worked out a valid method of determining it on the night of August 23, 1498. He used lunar observations and Ptolemy's 360 degrees for twenty four hours. He then figured the longitude by the number of hours it took to reach a certain point from a starting point. He had an almanac with him to give the movements of the moon. This lunar method of determining longitude was used by Captain Cook on his great round the world voyage in the 19th century and was the accepted way for three hundred years.

Amerigo by using the lunar method of determining longitude estimated the earth's circumference to be 24,852 English miles or just 50 miles less than what it is measured today.

The ship and its weary crew returned to Spain after the twenty days. They brought 200 natives that they captured home and sold them as slaves.

Chapter XX

Amerigo Returns From His Second Voyage

It was the year 1500. Amerigo and Giovanni were again on deck as their ship sailed up the Guadalquiver River to Seville. They had been gone for almost sixteen months on this, Amerigo's second voyage. It was the first for Giovanni. They were eagerly scanning the crowd on the river bank. "Would Maria, Luisa, and Pedro be on the dock to greet them?" Amerigo wondered.

The ship was just passing the Tower of Gold and the Alcazar Palace when suddenly Giovanni cried, "There they are!" as he spotted three people waving from the shore.

"Oh, it is Maria! Pedro and Luisa are with her," exclaimed Amerigo, and both waved back vigorously. It was the homecoming Amerigo had hoped for and young Giovanni shouted with glee.

After greeting Maria and his friends, Amerigo reported to Bishop Fonseca who passed on the report to King Ferdinand. Both realized that determining longitude was necessary to pin point the Line of Demarcation, the famous line drawn by the Pope to separate the Portuguese territory from that of Spain. Amerigo explained his lunar method for determining longitude. He also reported very strong equatorial currents and the discovery of the two great rivers.

Plans were soon being made for another voyage. "Do you have to go exploring again?" questioned Maria.

"You should be ashamed to go off and leave your newly made wife," chimed in Luisa.

"I am ashamed," confessed Amerigo. "I do realize that I'm not being fair to you, Maria, and what I'm planning now may pain you more."

Maria remained silent, waiting for Amerigo to go on but finally asked, "Why do you hesitate to tell me. Are you afraid to tell me?"

Amerigo smiled and replied, "I am conquering my fainting courage," teased Amerigo. "If my calculation of longitude is correct the Strait of Catigara must be in Portuguese waters. My next voyage may be from Portugal."

Maria rose to her feet__ "What!" she ejaculated, "From Portugal. That would make your absence longer."

"But I can see why it would be to Amerigo's advantage," said Pedro. "The Portuguese ships are larger and faster. Their seamen are better trained."

"Yes," agreed Amerigo. "Prince Henry, the Navigator, gave Portugal a head start in navigation. Spain will have to work hard to catch up."

"The discipline on board the Portuguese ships is better also," continued Pedro, "I understand that punishment is swift and sometimes severe. If a seaman falls asleep on his watch, he is put on a diet of bread and water. If this happens often or if this happens in the enemy's waters, he is stripped and flogged, and ducked three times. And you know how sailors hate water."

"When will you go?" questioned Luisa, ignoring Pedro's remarks.

"The date of the voyage has not been set but I have requested that it begin in May. That seems the best time to sail below the equator. There will be warmer weather and longer days," answered Amerigo.

"I thought it was always warm near the equator," put in Maria.

"It is," explained Amerigo, "but we plan to sail many degrees south of the equator. It will get colder and colder. If Ptolemy figured right the Strait of Catigara is eight and one half degrees south of the Tropic of Capricorn. We will be getting closer to the South Pole."

"But I thought it would be hotter there," said young Giovanni, who had been listening to the conversation.

"It would seem so but the South Pole is probably as cold as the North Pole. There is much you need to learn, Giovanni, and also much that scientist and all of us need to know about that unexplored part of the world," commented Amerigo.

Later when he and Maria were alone, Maria asked, "If the Portuguese are such good sailors why are they asking for your help?"

"King Emanuel has heard that I have determined a way to figure longitude. He wants to find out as accurately as possible where the Pope's Line of Demarcation is. That is the reason he is seeking my help," said Amerigo.

That evening when they were alone the conversation went on, "The thought of you going to sea again frightens me. I often wonder when you are away at sea whether you will ever return. The nights are long and lonely without you," said Maria with feeling.

"And I often wonder during those hellish storms at sea whether I'll ever get back to you, but something within me drives me on. I do so much want to be remembered for enlarging men's knowledge of the world. Please understand," pleaded Amerigo.

"And as I have told you, I do understand. My father and my first husband were also driven by such desires. I feared for them and now I fear for you. My nights are long and lonely as I lie here in bed alone, wondering if your mistress will ever let you come back to me."

"My mistress!" exclaimed Amerigo. "I have no mistress. I love only you."

Maria smiled and moved closer to him and murmured, "But Amerigo, you do have a mistress and one I can't compete with. Your mistress is the sea."

"Well," laughed Amerigo relieved. "She cannot snuggle up to me like you can. Her arms are cold and grasping. Yours are soft and loving. It is in your arms that I want to be," he then gathered her in his arms.

"Let us make the best of the time that we are together,"
suggested Maria. "In the morning I will make a picnic lunch and we'll
go down to the bank of the Guadalquiver River, just the two of us."

The next morning as they strolled along the bank of the
beautiful river, Amerigo observed, "It is amazing how much has been
found out about our world in the last half century. Prince Henry was
the one who began this era of exploration. He started a school for
navigators and encouraged voyages around Africa. By 1444, I have
read, his sea captains had sailed down the western coast of Africa as far
south as Sierra Leone. Gold was discovered and the Portuguese
continued to sail even farther South. Bartholomew Diaz rounded the
tip of Africa in 1488 and now Vasco de Gama has been to India."

"And Columbus has sailed straight west across the great Ocean
Sea," added Maria.

"Yes, and I expect Seville will be more affected by this great
discovery than any other city," added Amerigo. "It is an interesting
place to be. Most Florentines when away from Florence get homesick
for the sight of the Dome, the dome of our beautiful Cathedral, but
now when I am away, I dream of the graceful La Giralda Tower and
you. To return to Florence no longer excites me. It is here in Seville
with you that I want to spend the rest of my life."

"You say that," teased Maria, "as you, even now, are planning
to leave Seville and me for another voyage."

"But it is to you and to Seville that I will look forward to
coming home to. You are like the fragrant orange blossoms in your
garden. I often seem to get a faint scent of them when I'm far out on

the great water. My thoughts are of you and the beauty of the flowering almond, the brilliance of the large oleanders, the taste of the pomegranate. All are pleasant memories," he finished.

"And since you are waxing so poetic, don't forget the delicious taste of the ripe figs, the grapes, and the sweet chestnuts, but Spain, too, has prickly pears, and sometimes husbands are like prickly pears to their loving wives," teased Maria.

"You make me feel so guilty," said Amerigo contritely, "but someday you will be proud of me."

"I'm proud of you already," laughed Maria, "and again I say, I'd rather be proud of a live husband than one at the bottom of the sea."

"I'll come home safely," promised Amerigo. "But what is this that I hear about the Queen's order concerning gypsies?"

"It was in 1499, before you returned from your last voyage," answered Maria. "Queen Isabella ordered all gypsies to choose a fixed abode and to take to tilling the soil. She also demanded that they cease horse and cattle trading, and even ordered them to abandon their style of dress and their language."

"They will never obey her!" cried Amerigo. "What will become of my daughter and my granddaughter! Maybe I should give up my voyage and try to find them."

"But you won't," Maria prophesied, "I will look out for them, I promise."

Later, when again Maria and Amerigo were sauntering along

the river bank, Maria said thoughtfully, "You were on the high seas at midnight 1499, what if the world had come to an end! I couldn't help being uneasy. I wondered, just as most folks did about the end of the world. Now that was when I especially needed you."

Amerigo smiled, "That part of the chapter of Revelations has disturbed many. My uncle Giorgio said that in the year 999, the first millennium, everyone was very afraid. Many gave away all their possessions and spent the night in church praying. They even seemed disappointed that doomsday did not come. Still, even today at the end of every century there is much apprehension."

"How did the sailors on the ship act?" asked Maria. "Were they anxious?"

"You would have had to smile at the reaction as the midnight hour approached," recounted Amerigo. "Giovanni had reported to me about the uneasiness of the cabin boys, where upon I tried to explain to him and the other boys what had happened in 999, the first millennium. I told them what Uncle Giorgio had told me, and that even now people have the same fear at the end of each century that the end of the world will come. Four centuries had passed, I explained to them and nothing had happened."

"The boys thought it rather humorous and each tried to reassure their favorite sailor. Soon all were laughing and joking about it and all their fear seemed to disappear," explained Amerigo.

"On the eve of the year 1500, they all went to bed laughing and joking. I was on deck with Giovanni. It was his time to turn the ampoletta. As the midnight hour approached one by one the crew climbed aloft and without saying a word gazed at the stars. As we were approaching the equator, the North Star was very low in the sky.

I tried to explain that it was low because we were getting close to the equator. That even frightened them some more. They felt sure that the ship would sail over the edge of the world. They all dropped to their knees and their lips moved in prayer. They stayed in that pious position until Giovanni turned the midnight glass, and sang the usual ditty. One by one, they arose, each with a sheepish grin on their face and climbed back into bed," laughed Amerigo.

"But what did you do at midnight, Amerigo?" asked Maria.

"Well, I didn't want to be the only one standing so I, also fell to my knees and bowed my head in prayer," confessed Amerigo.

Chapter XXI

Amerigo's First Voyage for Portugal

It was the year 1501. Amerigo and his nephew, Giovanni were again on the high seas. It was Amerigo's third voyage and his first for Portugal. He had been invited by King Emanuel to come as an astronomer and a pilot. He was to use his knowledge of longitude to "nail down" the Line of Demarcation, the line proclaimed by Pope Alexander IV to separate the newly discovered land. All undiscovered lands east of this line would belong to Portugal and all lands west of it to Spain. This line was set at a distance 370 leagues west of the Cape Verde Islands.

This third voyage proved to be Amerigo's most important. He sailed along about six thousand miles of the coast of South America and realized that it had to be a fourth continent. He knew that the mainland of Asia did not extend below the equator and the enormous amount of fresh water gushing forth from the great rivers also indicated a great land mass. This continent was not known by the ancients. He announced this amazing discovery in a letter to his friend and patron, Lorenzo di Pier Francisco de Medici. This was welcome news in

Europe. Since news of the new discoveries was much sought after in the rest of Europe and as there were no newspapers, often letters were passed around. This letter, The Mundus Novus Letter, was printed on the newly invented printing press and was eagerly read. It was so in demand that thirteen editions were printed and circulated. Soon much of Europe was talking about the new continent. Scholars welcomed the news as did the common man. The feudal system was disintegrating and the freed serfs were looking for land of their own. Cities were crowded and offered only few ill-paying jobs. The new continent seemed to have been discovered at just the right time. More information about it was sought. Amerigo's Soderini Letter and others telling about the life of the native inhabitants, the great forest, the fertile soil, the brightly colored birds, also the animals and plants were soon printed and circulated. Columbus's letters, too, were printed and circulated but Amerigo's were more widely read.

Why was Amerigo able to recognize South America as a new continent? On his second voyage he had sailed along its coast from Venezuela to the eastern extent of the bulge of Brazil and on this third voyage he had continued sailing south to the islands now known as South Georgia 52 degrees south of the equator. In both voyages Amerigo had sailed along a total of 6000 miles of unbroken coast with no sign of Cathay or other known lands. It had to be a new continent. It could not be a part of Asia because Amerigo knew that Asia did not extend below the equator. This third voyage was also important for it proved that to reach India it would be necessary to sail around the southern tip of the new continent and possibly a new ocean might have to be crossed. It paved the way for Magellan's round-the-world voyage.

Gonzalo Coelho or Don Nuno Manuel may have been in command of this important voyage. After determining the Line of Demarcation, they were to explore the land discovered by Cabral and to report on the products deemed commercially profitable.

Three caravels made up the fleet and they had sailed from Lisbon on May 14, 1501. The first stop was the Cape Verde Islands located off the coast of Africa many miles south of the Azores. This became a convenient supply base for Portuguese ships bound for Brazil.

Amerigo noted in his letter to his patron, Lorenzo di Pier Francisco de Medici, that they encountered the Cabral's fleet returning from India. He listed the many and rare products that Cabral was bringing back from the Indies. The list included "an immense quantity of cinnamon, green and dry ginger, pepper, cloves, nutmeg, mace, musk, civet storax, benzoin, porcelain, cassia, incense, myrrh, red and white sandalwood, aloes, camphor, cypress, opium, and other drugs, as well as precious stones, including diamonds." His comment to his patron was "such a rich cargo will certainly prosper King Emanuel."

Amerigo also reported to Lorenzo the facts he learned in conversations with Cabral's guide and interpreter that would be of interest to commercial business. It was the desire for these riches that spurred the Spaniards on in the search for a strait that would reach India by sailing west. A route they believed would be shorter and less hazardous than the voyage around the Cape of Good Hope. Cabral had lost four ships in rounding the Cape of Good Hope. Indeed, it still was Cape Tormentos to sailing vessels. Santo Domingo on the island of Hispaniola was the first Spanish colony and it had been settled as a supply base for what was hoped to be a western water route to the Indies and was not expected to bring in any revenue. It would be years before the value of the Caribbean Islands would be realized.

After loading up supplies at Cape Verde, the three ships struggled through the usual belt of calms. Amerigo describes the weather during this period "as the vilest ever endured by man." It was hot and humid with a continuous drizzle often accompanied by fierce thunder and lightning. When the winds finally came they were brisk and the little fleet made the seven hundred leagues or 2100 English miles to the coast of Brazil in record time.

The landfall for this voyage was on the South American continent at the farthest east point of Brazil. Since it was sighted on the 16th of August, the festival day of Saint Roque, they named it San Roque. It retains the same name today.

The ships sailed southward following the coast. They often stopped to explore the country side and found similar natives as had been found by Columbus north of the equator. In some places they were friendly and in others the landing party was greeted with showers of arrows. These unfriendly natives quickly retreated with one shot from the ship's firearms.

The Indians as the natives came to be called were judged "wicked" by Amerigo for he judged them by Spanish customs. He wrote that it seemed that "All women were held in common, and they seemed to have no kings, no churches, or even idols. They do not carry on commerce or have money. They do," he added " carry on tribal warfare and kill and eat their enemy captives."

As the ships sailed southward the climate became more temperate similar to that of Spain. Birds of brilliant plumage and very tall trees were noted. Much logwood and aromatic herbs that could be of commercial value also seemed to thrive in that land.

"The ships cruised slowly" wrote Amerigo, "as if reluctant to leave this pleasant place." On the first of November right after All Saints Day, they entered a large bay that was named Bahia de Todas

Santos after the day. They continued their cruise and entered another large bay on New Year's Day. They mistook the bay for the mouth of another great river and named it Rio de Janeiro. Brazil's most important city was to grow up on that site. It still bears the name. The bay was later named the Guanabara Bay.

The ships cruised farther southward and westward until they reached a place on the coast that according to Amerigo's calculation was 370 leagues west of Cape Verde Islands. This they believed was the last land that Portugal could claim. There a marble slab four hands high, two hand wide, and one hand thick was placed to mark the Line of Demarcation. This according to Amerigo's calculation was 47 degrees 52 minutes west of Greenwich. This calculation was almost correct.

By the middle of February, the three ships had sailed past Cape Santa Maria and the land continued west of the Portuguese line. When they sighted the mouth of the great Rio de la Plata they decided to change directions, knowing for sure that they were out of Portuguese territory.

The ships set out into the open sea in a southeasterly direction thinking perhaps to find more islands belonging to Portugal. Before leaving the mainland the Portuguese captain surrendered the command of the fleet to Amerigo as he had been ordered not to sail in Spanish waters. From that time until the end of the voyage, Amerigo seemed in complete charge. He had the crew put in a six month supply of water and supplies.

They continued sailing in southeasterly direction. In March they were farther south than the Cape of Good Hope in Africa but even then they continued in the same direction. As they sailed farther to the south the nights grew longer and longer and the familiar constellations in the heavens disappeared. On April 3, the astrolabe reading showed latitude 52 degrees south. They continued south until a great storm arose on April 7th. For four days the ships were battered by fierce winds and for the four days they were compelled to sail under bare poles. Land was finally sighted at what was perhaps South Georgia. It was estimated to be 54 degrees south. The little ships, however, did not dare land for the coast was "more forbidding than the sea." It was a "dreadful coast" with glaciers coming down to the water's edge.

As soon as the three ships were able to exchange signals, it was decided to head for home. Amerigo was still in charge of navigation. He headed in a northeasterly direction straight to Sierra Leone on the African coast. The distance across the open sea was approximately 4000 miles. This little fleet had already sailed along thousands of miles of the South American coast. Much of it's coast would soon be accurately mapped from his findings.

As they sailed toward Africa, they sailed on calmer seas and Amerigo could continue Giovanni's education. There was ample time during the long Antarctic nights to study the heavens. Night after night, they searched for a south pole star, but found none but noted again the four stars that came to be known as The Southern Cross. They seemed to be in a fixed position.

Giovanni was an eager learner and often the lesson began with a question. "Who was Ptolemy?" he asked, "and why do you believe so fervently in his teachings. Didn't he live many centuries ago?"

"Yes," replied Amerigo, "He lived in the second century. Many wise men in those times had studied astronomy. The heavens were of early interest to the ancients. They sought to understand the movements of the stars, the sun, the winds, and the clouds. This knowledge was used by early sailors to guide ships out of the sight of land. They also studied about all the continents then known, Europe, Asia, and Africa. Ptolemy collected all their findings in his book The Almagest. In it he systematized and recorded all data known to men up to that time."

"But wasn't more knowledge accumulated during the thousands of years between then and now?" wondered Giovanni.

"Not much of value seemed to have been learned during all these years. When the Great Roman Empire fell there was much disorder. Much knowledge of the past was lost and very little new was learned. We were lucky that the Arabs who conquered Alexandria and Egypt saved some valuable manuscripts of the ancients. These manuscripts were housed in the famous university in Alexandria, Egypt. Slowly some of these manuscripts made their way to the west but it was not until the Fall of Constantinople that their importance was realized. Many scholars of that great city were forced to western Europe and they brought the ancient manuscripts and knowledge with them," explained Amerigo.

"What did Ptolemy teach that you consider so important?" was the next question.

"He taught that the earth was round like a great globe. He also believed that the earth was the center of the universe and that all the heavenly bodies revolved around it in a fixed orbit," explained Amerigo, "but the part of his Almagest that fascinated me most is his methods of determining latitude and longitude. He used Babylonian mathematics and figured that if all circles have 360 degrees, the earth being a great ball or globe also must have 360 degrees. By using 360 degrees as the distance around the globe, Ptolemy devised a satisfactory way to determine latitude. He did not, however, live long enough to devise a satisfactory way to determine longitude. He challenged future scientist to find a better way and I am seeking to find a better way," finished Amerigo.

"Now, I'm beginning to understand," said Giovanni. "During all those long nights on our other voyage that is what you were searching for."

"And on this voyage, I intended to sail far enough to the south to find what Ptolemy believed to be a strait that would connect the two great bays," continued Amerigo. "He called the strait, The Strait of Catigara." The weather, however, and the danger of our ships being eaten up by teredo worms has forced us to turn back."

"It has been a long voyage. It will be good to get home," agreed Giovanni.

"The more I study longitude, I have come to believe that a degree is longer than that figured by Ptolemy or any of the ancients. I believe Toscanelli's estimate is more accurate, and certainly more accurate than Columbus's.

"How many miles do you now estimate to be a degree?" asked Giovanni.

"Columbus estimated a degree to be 56 2/3 Roman miles (52 English). I now believe it to be nearer 75 (69 English). That would make the earth much larger than estimated. I now estimate the earth's circumference at the equator to be near 27,000 Roman miles (24,852 English). Columbus estimated it to be 20,400 Roman miles (English 18,720)," explained Amerigo.

"That is a big difference. No wonder he thinks he has reached the Indies!" exclaimed Giovanni.

"During this voyage it has become evident that we have not reached Asia but are sailing along the coast of a new continent, a continent not known by Ptolemy or any of the ancients," Amerigo said seriously.

"A new continent, how exciting!" exclaimed Giovanni.

"And now I have decided that the Strait of Catigara is not in Portuguese territory. We now must return to Spain for it must be on the Spanish side of the Line of Demarcation," added Amerigo. However I have contracted for another voyage with King Emanuel. After that we return to Spain."

"I'm sure Aunt Maria will be glad to hear that," said Giovanni thoughtfully, "and I am too."

"And I will add my name to that list," laughed Amerigo. "It will be good to be in Seville again."

The reader may be interested to know that a degree is 75.15 Roman miles and the circumference of the earth is now estimated to be 27,054 (24,901 English). Amerigo's estimate was only 54 miles short.

The return voyage across the vast south Atlantic of four thousand miles was evidently blessed with favorable winds and fair weather for it was made in record time. This voyage is considered by many to be the most extraordinary feat of navigation since Columbus's first voyage. At Sierra Leone on the coast of Africa, one of the caravels of the little fleet had to be abandoned for it was no longer sea worthy. The other two sailed north to Lisbon by way of the Azores Islands.

King Emanuel did not understand the significance of this

voyage or its historical importance. Even though the purpose of it was to discover and explore, he was disappointed that the returning cargo contained no gold or precious stones but only logwood, parrots and monkeys.

The following letter was waiting for Amerigo when he returned to Seville. He immediately posted a reply. Both are as follows:

Florence 1502

Dear Amerigo, my deserving nephew,

It must be about time for you to return from your voyage for Portugal. Hope you found Ptolemy's Strait of Catigara as you hoped. From what I've heard from you and from other sources it does seem that a vast amount of land has been discovered and none of it faintly evenly resemble any of the coast of Asia that we have read about. Certainly there must be a strait somewhere in that vast expanse of land that will take you to India, the land that you seek. Please keep me informed as to what you have found.

Here in Florence things are happening fast. There have been three deaths that greatly grieve our family and will greatly grieve you and Giovanni. His mother Catarina died, and so did Guido Antonio, and so did your patron, Lorenzo di Pier Francisco de Medici. I know their death will greatly sadden you. In fact all Florence weeps for them.

We hope, however, for better times. Your friend, Piero Soderini, has at last agreed to serve as gonfaloniere. He was sworn in 1501. He may not be as wise and certainly not as forceful as Guido, but he seems to be following a middle of the road policy, a policy that seems to be sensible for

Florence at this time. It is even now being considered to make him gonfaloniere for life. I saw him recently and he asked about you and was sincerely interested in your voyages.

We will be anxiously awaiting your account of your last voyage.

With thoughts and prayers of you and Giovanni's safety,

Your loving uncle,
Giorgio Antonio

Lisbon 1502

To my dearest uncle Giorgio Antonio:

Giovanni and I were much grieved at the news of his mother's death. She was a faithful wife to Antonio. The sad news of Guido's death also made me realize how far I am from my loved ones. The news, too, of Lorenzo di Pier Francisco de Medici's death was awaiting me at the port when I returned. We are indeed bereaved.

All this sad news makes my voyage unimportant but nevertheless I will report to you. It was a long and eventful journey. We journeyed southwest for 64 days and made landfall south of the equator, probably about 5 degrees south of it. Soon the little dipper (Ursa Minor) and the big dipper (Ursa Major) became invisible to us. The purpose of this voyage was mainly for geographical purposes, not commercial. We were to establish the location of the Line of Demarcation as set by the pope. King Emanuel seems more interested in exploration than King Ferdinand.

Since it was San Roque's Day when we made landfall we called it Cape San Roque. We sailed many leagues along the coast. It was pleasant to go on land. The gentle breezes and the exotic odors of fruit contrasted with the awful smell of the ship, the molding hard tack, the sour smell of the olives, and the musty sails. A caravel after months at sea "is like a cellar . . . a better habitat for rats than for men."

This land contained much logwood or Brazil wood so we called it, Brazil. A certain wealthy and converted Jew, Fernand de Noronha, outfitted one of our ships. We filled it with a load of logwood and returned it to Portugal early.

We cruised slowly along the coast stopping at a cape we called Cabo Santo Agostinko and then on to the mouth of a beautiful river. We called it Rio de Janeiro because we reached it on News Year's Day, Jan. 1, 1501.

Ptolemy's Strait of Catigara continues to elude us, but we have come to the conclusion that we have been sailing along a new continent. A continent that was not known to the ancients. We are sure that the earth is larger than Ptolemy ever dreamed. It may be even larger than your friend Toscanelli estimated and much larger than Columbus thought. Ptolemy estimated the circumference to be 22,500 Roman miles, Columbus estimated it to be only 20,400. He thought Asia extended much farther east than the others believed. Now, I have decided that a degree instead of being 56 and 2/3 miles is closer to 75 Roman miles. That would make the earth circumference 27,000 Roman miles. What do you believe?

I believe also that there is another ocean to cross before reaching Asia. I will be interested in your opinion.

Your nephew,
Amerigo

Chapter XXII

Columbus's High Voyage

It was 1502. Columbus had continued to follow the Royal Court around petitioning the sovereigns for complete restoration of his rights, properties, titles, and offices. It was not until September 1501, when Don Nicolas de Ovando had been appointed Governor of the Islands and Mainland of the Indies that Columbus finally realized that he would not be allowed to return to Hispaniola. He was allowed to retain his titles of Viceroy and Admiral and was given permission to send an envoy to Santo Domingo to collect the moneys owed him. Ovando with thirty ships and 2500 sailors, soldiers, and colonist set sail in February 1502. One ship, under the command of Carvajal, was sent by Columbus to pick up his gold.

Columbus then petitioned for permission to go exploring again. He was speedily given four caravels and set sail from Seville on April 1, 1502. This voyage Columbus called El Alto Viaje, The High Voyage, and it was to test all his perseverance and courage. The little fleet was plagued by a hurricane, many tropical storms, and ended with a year marooned on Jamaica. There he was further tested by a mutiny of a dissatisfied few.

On this, his fourth voyage, Columbus was determined to find the strait that separated the lower province of China from India for he still believed that Cuba was a part of the Chinese province of Mangi. Bartholomew Columbus, his older brother, came along on this voyage. Columbus also took his younger son, Ferdinand, who many years later, wrote a biography of his father, and from it we have a detailed record of this voyage and indeed it proved to be one of high adventure.

Columbus followed the path of his second voyage in crossing the great Ocean Sea. His first landfall was the island of Martinique. There he tarried for a few days for water and rest before heading for Santo Domingo on the island of Hispaniola. He had strict orders not to stop there from King Ferdinand and Queen Isabella but he had three good reasons for doing so at the time. He had enough experience in the Caribbean to recognize that a hurricane was brewing. He needed a safe harbor for his ships. He also knew that many of Ovando's large fleet would be soon returning to Spain; he wanted to warn him of the possibility of the hurricane; he also hoped to exchange one of his four ships for a better one, and to send some letters home.

Columbus sent Pedro de Terreros with a message to Governor Ovando. Ovando refused his request and ignored his warning and his large fleet of almost of almost thirty caravels set sail for Spain the next day. The hurricane struck as Columbus had predicted, nineteen ships sank with all hands on board, six others were lost but a few of their crew survived, four ships returned to Santo Domingo in a sinking condition. Only one made it safely through the storm to Spain. Interestingly, it was the one commanded by Columbus's agent, Carvajal, carrying Columbus's gold. It was estimated that more than a half million dollars in gold went to the bottom of the sea on the sunken ships.

After being refused permission to moor his ships in the harbor of Santo Domingo, Columbus quickly steered his ships toward the mouth of the Rio Jaina but the hurricane winds drove them out to sea. They rode out the storm safely, however, and rejoined each other at the designated place.

Columbus and his crew gave thanks to God for delivering them from the storms and rested for about ten days. Then they began their long search for the hoped for strait. They sailed across the Windward Passage to the south shore of Cuba, down to Jamaica, then across the open sea for more than three hundred miles. They skirted the northern coast of what is now Honduras, staying close to the shore hoping to find the looked for strait. The rainy season came and brought a deluge of rain and hot steamy weather. Mosquitoes and the tossing of the ships kept them awake at night. The current and winds were so contrary that only a very few leagues could be made each day. Columbus wrote "What man ever born, not excepting Job, would not have died of despair when in such weather, seeking safety for son, brother, shipmates and myself, we were forbidden the land and harbor that I by God's will and sweating blood, won for Spain!"

With singleness of purpose and perseverance, Columbus, though often sick, sailed on. They, at last, reached the eastern most point of Honduras and rounded a cape that Columbus called Gracias a Dios (Thanks be to God) for there the coast turned southward and the winds became favorable.

They continued the voyage southward along the coast of Nicaragua and Costa Rica still searching for "the strait." Often the ships anchored to trade with the Indians. Some had gold mixed with copper, the guanin, that Seville jewelers had declared of little value. Later and farther south they did find pure gold. They sailed through a channel into a large bay, the channel Columbus called Boca del

Dragon, because of it's dangerous current, the bay is now named Almirante Bay after Columbus. On the shore of the bay they found Indians wearing disks of fine gold and traded three hawk's bells for each disk. The bells were worth about a penny apiece.

While there they learned from the Indians that this was an isthmus with a large body of water on the other side. They found no strait and high mountains blocked their way across. It was now November, more heavy rains came, the men were exhausted, the food "foul and full of weevils." They spent "a miserable Christmas" in the harbor of what is now Cristobal in the Panama Canal Zone. They were close to the Pacific but unable to cross the jungle. It would be left to Balboa about a decade later to be the first to see that broad ocean. He and his men starting fresh at the Atlantic side were able to cut their way through the insect infested jungle. Columbus's men would not have survived such a venture.

After the first of the year the small fleet retraced their steps up the Veragua coast. Columbus's purpose now was to find a suitable site for a trading post. Soon they reached the mouth of a river. Since the water across its bar was about seven feet deep, they towed the ships across and anchored them in a large basin of water. All the Indians along the coast wore gold ornaments. Columbus felt sure that much gold could be mined on the river banks and because the Indian cacique, Quibian, seemed friendly, he decided to build the trading post there.

A fort and a dozen thatched huts were built and plans were made for Bartholomew Columbus to stay at this fort with twenty men. The ship Gallega would be left for them.

Quibian, the Indian cacique, was friendly enough but only when he thought the visitors were temporary. When he realized they were preparing to stay, he began preparing for battle. When this change of attitude became apparent, a Spanish gentleman, Diego Mendez, showed the courage and resourcefulness that saved the day, not only then but many times in the future. He with a companion, Rodrigo de Escobar, in order to pacify the menacing Indians, walked bravely to the Indian camp, took out his barber's kit, and had his companion cut his hair. The cacique, Quibian, was so impressed that he asked for his hair to be trimmed. After cutting Quibian's hair, Mendez graciously presented the barber's kit to the cacique. Peace seemed to be made but not for long. Columbus decided to capture the cacique and hold him as hostage.

Diego Mendez lead the attack and Quibian was captured with about twenty of his men. They also took many gold objects from the Indians. The wily cacique somehow managed to escape. He quickly rallied his enraged men against the little garrison. Columbus and his crew were in the process of towing the three caravels across the bar when the Indians, four hundred strong, attacked. They were beaten off with the help of the great wolfhound. The loss was great however for the captain of the flagship, Tristan, was killed along with ten other Spaniards. It was decided then to abandon the fort altogether, but since the water across the bar was too shallow, they had to leave the Gallega behind. It was one of their better ships.

Diego Mendez again showed his resourcefulness. He built a raft and brought most of the gold and supplies from the Gallega to the other side of the bar. Columbus then made Diego Mendez, captain of his flagship, the Capitana, and again they set sail westward and northward. They left that "miserable place" wrote Samuel Eliot Morison "on Easter Sunday April 16, 1503, and today that site remains as wild and wet and forbiddingly beautiful as when Columbus landed there on the Feast of the Three Kings" in 1503.

This place Columbus called Belen but it was not the present

day Belen, which is located near the mouth of the Amazon River. Columbus only sailed as far as the Gulf of Darien on this voyage. He only reached the continent of South America briefly and that was on his third voyage. This may have been the reason Columbus's sons never disputed the name AMERICA during Columbus and Amerigo's lifetime. The name was only given at that time to what is now known as Brazil. It was many years later before Mercator put the name on both continents. Not even during the Probansas, the long lawsuit filed against the crown by the Columbus's son, Diego, was any word ever raised against Amerigo.

Columbus aimed to reach the harbor at Santo Domingo but reckoned wrong. The ships despite being tar coated before leaving Spain were "riddled by teredo worms." The smallest ship had to be abandoned and the crew divided between the other two. Even then all hands were kept busy pumping and bailing out water. The best Columbus could do to save all lives aboard was to head for Jamaica. The ships were in no condition to buck the head winds for the additional hundred miles to Hispaniola.

The Capitana and the Bermuda were in a sinking condition when they reached Jamaica. Columbus ordered both to be run aground on a sandy beach of the island. Palm beach huts were built on their decks for shelter from the blistering sun and pouring rain. There for more than a year remained the one hundred and sixteen men left alive. Rescue, Columbus knew, would be slow in coming, if at all, for he had let it be known that there was no gold on Jamaica. Luckily there was an Indian village near by and again Diego Mendez was of service, he was sent there to get provisions. Columbus, through Mendez, then drew up a contract with the Indians to furnish food for the starving crew. The Indians would be paid with glass beads and the usual hawk's bells.

Hispaniola was only one hundred and eight miles to the east but it was across the open sea. Again Diego Mendez saved the day. He bought a large dugout canoe from the Indians, fitted it out with sails, loaded it with water and provision, and set sail for Hispaniola. This attempt failed for the Indians captured Mendez. He, however, managed to escape and soon another attempt was planned. Two canoes this time were fitted out with sails, Mendez would pilot one and Bartolomeo Fieschi was to pilot the other. They set sail across the 108 miles of open water. It was an arduous trip for in the daytime sun scorched them. The boats were able to make only one mile and hour. Luckily they encountered an island seventy eight miles out where they rested and obtained water. From this small island they observed the high mountains of Hispaniola. With renewed hope and after a much needed rest the two canoes laboriously made their way to the coast of Hispaniola. Mendez requested a ship to rescue Columbus but Ovando kept putting him off.

While back in Jamaica, Columbus waited and prayed. Seven months passed and no word had been heard from Mendez and his men. Columbus and his remaining sailors had no way of knowing whether they had reached Hispaniola. It was the lowest point of the voyage. Forty-eight men mutinied and taking canoes headed toward Hispaniola. A brisk wind drove them back. They, then, roved the island robbing the Indians. The outraged savages, who now had more than enough hawk's bells and were tired of bringing food to the Spaniards, refused to bring more. It was at this time that Columbus staged his famous eclipse trick. He had brought along an almanac that predicted a total eclipse of the moon on February 29,1504. He summoned the Indian caciques and told them that the great God was angry with them for refusing to bring food to his starving envoys. He would give them a warning sign. They were told to watch the moon that night. When the moon rose, it was partly in eclipse, and the darkness gradually increased. The terrified Indians begged Columbus to intercede for them. Columbus promised to do so and went back into his cabin to pray. When the eclipse was total, he emerged and told the Indians that God had heard his prayers and if they promised to bring food, the terrible calamity would not occur. They promised and the Spaniards had no more trouble with their food supply.

In March 1504, eight months after Mendez and his men had set out, a small Spanish ship appeared in the harbor to bring a message that Mendez was doing his best to charter a ship to rescue them. It was a small ship and no one was allowed to return on it but it did bring some saltpork and some casks of wine. The rescue ship finally came in June and took the remaining crew back to Hispaniola. There Columbus charted a caravel and after a stormy voyage finally reached Spain in November 1504. This fourth voyage ended after two and one half years. No strait had been found, no trading post had been established, and his letter to the court was unanswered for the queen lay on her death bed. Columbus rented a house in Seville. He was too ill to go to the court even if he had been summoned. It was at this Seville house that Amerigo would later visit him.

Chapter XXIII

Amerigo's Fourth Voyage

It was the year 1503. Amerigo made a brief visit to Seville after the 1501- 1502 voyage to see Maria and his friends. He brought the news that he was committed to another voyage for Portugal. The aim of this voyage was to search for a strait that would take him to the Island of Malacca, an island known to be rich in spices. Much of this voyage was to be financed by a converted wealthy Jew. His purpose, different from the King's, was to find a satisfactory site for a colony for his fellow Jews and where logwood could be cut and made ready to be loaded for future ships.

Fernand de Noronha, the wealthy converted Jew, had furnished a ship for Amerigo's first voyage for Portugal. It had been returned early to Lisbon loaded with logwood. Noronha was quick to realize the value of this wood for making washable red, blue, and black dye for the textile business. He quickly contracted with King Emanuel for a ten year monopoly of this valuable wood for four thousand ducats a year.

Unlike the Spanish, Portugal needed more citizens so instead of exile, King Emanuel decreed compulsory baptism for all Jews between the age of four and twenty-four. He thus added to Portugal 20,000 new citizens within a month. Fernand de Noronha represented an affluent group of Jews. He feared for the unconverted ones so he made provisions for a colony in the new land. His fears were well founded for the very next year under pressure from the Spanish sovereigns all unconverted Jews were expelled from Portugal.

Soon six ships were readied for this voyage for Portugal. Gonzalo Coelho was in command of this fleet. The first stop was at Serra Leone on the coast of Africa, which became a customary supply base for Portuguese ships bound for Brazil. They took on supplies and sailed west by south. They stopped for water at a small island in the mid Atlantic. On it they found fresh water and birds so tame they could be picked up by hand but no native inhabitants. The island was only two leagues long and one league wide. This may have been Ascension Island or one that has long since disappeared. On this island one ship struck a reef and went down but all her crew were saved. Coelho sent Amerigo on to find a harbor off the coast of Brazil. Amerigo found one located where today is the great city of Bahia. He waited seventeen days for the fleet before one ship showed up. They together waited two more months for the others and decided that it was futile to wait longer. It was figured that the others were lost at sea.

The ships took on water and wood and sailed leisurely down the coast until they reached another harbor at Cape Frio. Here, it was decided, would be a good location for the trading post. They loaded the ships with logwood and built a fort. They left there the twenty-four men who were survivors of the sunk ship. They were to cut logwood and have a load ready for the next ship that Noronha would send out. This became the first Portuguese settlement in Brazil. Much of the logwood harvested by Fernand de Noronha was cut from this settlement and from the island cited off the coast of Brazil. That island was named for Noronha and still bears his name.

A strait that would take them to the spice islands was not found. So much time had been lost waiting for the fleet, building the fort, cutting logwood, and since the ships were not in good shape to travel farther, they headed straight for Lisbon. They arrived in Lisbon on the eighth of June 1504. Amerigo turned his charts and maps over to King Emanuel expecting to have them returned. Fernand de Noronha was pleased with the logwood and with the news of the colony. It is not known whether the Jews were ever able to settle there. The next year was the year all unconverted Jews were exiled at the urging of the Spanish crown. Most of them went to Holland.

Amerigo tarried in Portugal waiting for the maps and charts to be returned for now he had determined to return to Spain. He was sure that any strait around the continent would be on the Spanish side of the Line of Demarcation. While waiting for his maps and charts he wrote his famous letter to Piero Soderini and mailed it from Lisbon. Excerpts from the letter are included here. The letter began with the usual flowing salutation.

Most Excellent Sir:

I would impart to your Excellency a description of things seen by me in various climes, in the course of the four voyages I have made for the discovery of new lands, two by the authority and command of Don Ferdinand VI, King of Castile, in the great western ocean and two other by order of King Emanuel, King of Portugal toward the south. . . . King Ferdinand of Castile had ordered four ships to go in search of new lands, and I was selected by His Majesty to go in that fleet to assist in the discoveries. We sailed from the good port of Cadiz on the tenth day of May, A. D. 1497, and steering our course through the great Western Ocean, spent eighteen months on our expedition, discovering much land and a great number of islands, the largest part of which were inhabited. As these people (the Indians) are not spoken of by the ancients, I promise they were ignorant of them. If I am not mistaken I well remember that this ocean was considered unpeopled: and our poet Dante also held this opinion, judging by the twenty-sixth canto of L'Inferno, where he sings the fate of Ulysses. In this voyage I saw many astonishing things as your Excellency will perceive by the following revelation:

. . . We sailed so rapidly, that at the end of twenty seven days we came in sight of land, which we judged to be a continent, being about a thousand leagues (3000 miles) west of the Grand Canaries, and within the Torrid Zone . . . as we found the North Star at an elevation of six degrees above the horizon . . . .. Here we anchored our ships a league and a half from shore: and having cast off our boats, proceeded at once to land.

Before we landed we were much cheered by the sight of many people rambling along the shore. We found that they were all in a state of nudity, and appeared afraid of us, as I suppose seeing us clothed, and of a different statue, they retreated to the mountain and not withstanding all our signs of peace we could not bring them to parley with us; so as night was coming on, and the ships were anchored in an unsecured place, by reason of the coast being exposed. We agreed to leave the next day and go in search of some bay where we could place our ships in safety.

We sailed along the coast with a northeast wind, always keeping within sight of land, and continually seeing people on shore: and having sailed two days, we found a safe place at half a league from land, the same day we landed our boats, forty men leaping on shore in good order. The people of the country, however appeared very shy of us and for sometime we could not sufficiently assure them . . . to come and speak with us: but at length we labored so hard giving them some of our things, such as looking glasses, bells, beads, and other trifles, that some of them acquired confidence enough to come and treat us with our mutual peace and friendship. Night coming on we took leave of them and returned to our ships.

The next day as the dawn appeared, we saw on the shore a great number with their wives and children; we landed and found that they had all come loaded with provision and material, which I will describe in a proper place. Before we reached land many swam to meet us, the length of a bow shot from the sea, (as they are most excellent swimmers) and they treated us with much confidence as if we had intercourse with them for a long time, which gratified us very much.

All that we know of their life and manners is that they go entirely naked not having the slightest covering whatever; they are of middling statue, and very well proportioned; their flesh is of a reddish color, like the skin of a lion, but I think if they had been accustomed to wearing clothing, they would have been as white as we are. They have no hair on their body, with the exception of long hair upon their heads . . . and the women especially derive much beauty from this; their countenances are not very handsome as they have large faces, which might be compared to that of the Tartars; they do not allow any hair to grow on their eye brows, or any other part of the body except the head, as they consider it a great deformity. Both women and men are very agile and easy in their person, and swift in walking and swimming, the women think nothing of running a league or two, as we many times beheld, having in this particular, greatly the advantage of us, Christians.

. . . These people have no captains, neither do they march in order, but each one is his own master . . . . . They sleep in nets of cotton, very large and suspended from the air, and although this may seem a bad way of sleeping, I can vouch for the fact that it is extremely pleasant and one sleeps better than on a mattress . . . . .

. . . They eat little meat except human flesh . . . . .

. . . We found that these people make bread of small fish, which they have caught in the sea, by first boiling them and then kneading them together and making a paste of them, which they baked upon hot coals; we tried them and found them good . . . . .

Amerigo seemed to have an eye for detail and his writings delighted the Europeans. He even described their sexual habits. His writings were read more than those of Columbus and his name became well known.

King Emanuel did not return his maps and charts. For he declared that all such maritime charts made while on a voyage in Portuguese waters belonged to the crown. On learning this, Amerigo and Giovanni set sail for Spain.

Chapter XXIV

Queen Isabella and Spain

It was the year 1504. This was a year of sadness in Spain. Isabella's illness and her death in November left a place that would be hard to fill. She and Ferdinand had made a good team. They complemented each other and although they often disagreed they had respect for each other's opinions and considered both opinions when making a decision. Ferdinand led the successful fight against the Moors but it was probably Isabella's determination to win that drove him on. She also collected the money to wage war. Columbus may not have sailed if it had been up to Ferdinand but he assented for he respected her judgement. Again if it had been left up to Ferdinand the Jews may not have been expelled but again he bowed to her wishes. The decision to back Columbus was a wise one but the decision to expel the Jews proved unwise. This pius Queen, however, wanted to rule over a completely Christian people.

Isabella and Ferdinand were married for 35 years and although they worked together well, Isabella's life with him was not smooth. During their marriage, Ferdinand fathered four illegitimate children, two girls and two boys. Each had a different mother. He had no steady mistress. The girls were tucked away in a convent; one son became a soldier, and the other at age six was made archbishop of Zaragoza. When Cardinal Mendoza died, Ferdinand wanted to make him archbishop of Toledo which would have made him the prime religious figure in Spain. Isabella did not allow it. Francisco Jimenez de Cisneros was appointed to that important position and when Isabella died he was strong enough to hold Spain together for Ferdinand. Jimenez proved to be a wise choice. One of Isabella's strengths as queen was her ability to choose able men to assist the governing.

Isabella faced bravely her many family tragedies. Her son, the crown prince, Juan died and his death was soon followed by that of his infant son. Her eldest daughter, Isabella, died soon afterward as did her infant daughter and Isabella had to leave her crown to her other daughter, Joanna, who was mentally unstable. She did fortunately for Spain provide that Ferdinand be regent.

Isabella's official title was long. It was Queen Isabella of Castile, the first lady of Aragon, of Sicily, Galicia, Majorea, Gilbratar, Rounllon, Sardinia and Biscay . . . and even more. She ruled with graciousness (con blandura). Graciously she welcomed troops, graciously she distributed alms, graciously but firmly she forbid the service of prostitutes for the army. Her conversation was "sometimes gay" but mostly she was serious. Her manner, however, was always "with unruffled composure." She improved education for Spain and especially for women. The university at Seville was established in 1502, as well as, schools in other places of learning. She ruled when nation states were emerging. Before her time Spain and much of Europe was a hodge podge of Dukedoms, often warring one another. Isabella left Spain well on the way to becoming a unified nation and the strongest one in Europe. Her reign with Ferdinand ushered in Spain's Golden Age.

This eulogy was written at her death by a devoted courtier.

The pen falls from my hand and strength fails me through grief. The world has lost its most precious ornament, and the loss should be moaned, not only by Spaniards who she so long led, but by all the nations of Christendom, because she was the mirror of all virtues, the refuge of the innocent, and the scourge of the evil. I doubt that there has lived in this world, a heroine, either in ancient or modern times who merits comparison with the peerless woman.

Queen Isabella died in Medina del Campo in November 1504. Her body was embalmed and clad in a simple Franciscan robe as a shroud and was borne on a black litter to Granada. The following moving description of its journey to its final resting place was written by the early historian, Bartholome de las Casas.

From the moment the cavalcade set out from Medina, one gloomy November day, it moved through a wild storm of wind and rain all the way to Granada. In many places the roads were impassable, the swollen streams having washed the bridges away, and little brooks had grown to the volume of the Tagus (river), while low lying plains had been converted into lakes . . . . . Neither the sun or the stars were visible during the three weeks of the journey. Raging torrents at times swept away horses and mules, and some of the riders were lost too . . . . . People screamed with woe, women tore their hair, and the churches echoed with solemn chant. The procession, garbed in black at the on set of the journey arrived at the destination caked in mud. In this manner the bones of the Queen arrived at the monastery of San Francisco of the Alhambra, to rest in a setting of Moorish associations.

Isabella's last words to Ferdinand were "I beseech the King, my Lord, that he be pleased to accept my jewels and belongings, or such as he likes best, that seeing them he will be reminded of the singular love I always felt for his lordship, and even so, that he may ever bear in mind that he is to die and I will be waiting for him in the other life, with which memory he may live more purely and justly."

With the death of Isabella, Columbus had lost his best friend. She had many times held out a helping hand to him. Ferdinand assumed the regency in the name of Queen Joanna the Mad.

Chapter XXV

Amerigo Returns to Spain

It was still the year 1504. After King Emanuel refused to return his maps and charts, Amerigo and his nephew, Giovanni, returned to Spain. As they were again sailing up the Guadalquiver River the Torre del Oro, shining golden in the sunlight came into view, then the mighty Alcazar Palace Fortress, followed by the graceful Giralda. Giovanni, who was then a lad of seventeen, said to Amerigo, "Seville has a cathedral palace, and a bell tower like ours in Florence. They are also beautiful but are quite different."

"Yes," agreed Amerigo. "They are different for most were built by the Moors. They occupied much of Spain for about 700 years and brought oriental ideas to Spain. The Alcazar Palace reflects their architecture, as well as, that of Spain. It is a magnificent structure. No one has ever been sure how many rooms are in it."

"Is the Alcazar Palace in Seville as wonderful as the Alhambra?" asked Giovanni. "Aunt Maria has told me that the Alhambra is the most beautiful building in Spain."

"And no doubt it is," responded Amerigo, "but the Seville Alcazar is still a captivating palace."

"The name Alcazar puzzles me. In Cordoba there is also a palace named Alcazar," stated Giovanni.

"Yes, " replied his uncle, "The Moors built fortress palaces in every large city in Spain and they are all still called the Alcazar, which is the Moorish name for such a structure."

Giovanni continued to gaze at the skyline of Seville and Amerigo remained deep in thought as the ship slowly made its was up to the docks, and after a time said, "I am glad you are interested in Seville and Spain. I have been fascinated by it since my first arrival. Now I feel like it is my home. I hope you will come to feel the same way."

Suddenly Giovanni cried out, "There they are, but who is the young woman with Maria?"

Quickly Amerigo looked in the direction to which he was pointing, "Yes that is Maria," he said, "But I do not recognize her companion."

They were soon to know for after he and Maria had embraced, she turned to the young woman and said, "Amerigo, this is your granddaughter. She has come to live with us."

The astonished Amerigo looked into the solemn brown eyes that were looking up at him expectantly. "Yes, she has Elena's beautiful eyes," he thought. "My dear," he said, "This is a wish come true, I have wished so much to find you."

Later Maria explained to him that his daughter, Elena, had come to Seville searching for him. She had learned at the waterfront that Amerigo was away at sea and he had a wife. She sought out Maria and told her why she had come.

"Since the decree of the Sovereigns concerning gypsies, I have been very uneasy about my daughter's future. We, gypsies, can never conform to the harsh laws against us. We have been continually on the move and fear we may be thrown in prison or even possibly confronted by the Inquisador," she said.

"Yes, we have been concerned about you," said Maria.

"Little Elena," she continued, "seems more Florentine than gypsy. In that way she is different from my mother and me, so I decided to bring her to her grandfather, Amerigo."

"I know Amerigo will be happy and pleased," Maria had answered quickly as she put her arm around the young Elena. "He has told me about you and said he had begged you both to come with him to Spain. Amerigo will, I hope, be home soon and meanwhile young Elena can stay with me."

Very much relieved Amerigo's daughter left her young daughter with Maria and went back to her gypsy husband and to her gypsy life.

It was a happy homecoming for Amerigo. He and Maria with Giovanni and the young Elena, now in her teens, settled down to live as a family.

"Now," Maria said, "We have a son and a daughter. We are blessed."

"I am the one blessed," replied Amerigo, "to have a wife like you. You are an understanding and a giving woman. My love and respect for you grows each day and there are many other things I need to say."

"Hush," laughed Maria. "You are waxing poetic again. Now tell me about your voyage and your future plans."

"I hope they will please you," replied Amerigo seriously. "When I was reporting to Bishop Fonseca, he suggested that I apply for Spanish citizenship. I am seriously considering that for now I feel more Spanish than Florentine and I want to spend the rest of my life in Seville."

"That is something I have longed to hear," Maria said quietly. "Often I have heard you say, 'That a Florentine might roam but always he finally returns to Florence,' but now I have another rival, the sea? Will she beckon you again?"

"Perhaps," he smiled, but added to reassure her, "If I do I will sail for Spain. I still would like to discover Ptolemy's Strait of Catigara. After sailing along what I believe to be a new continent, much of it is south of the equator, I am sure that such a strait if it exist, will be on the Spanish side of the Line of Demarcation."

"So its not just your love of me and Spain that keeps you here," teased Maria.

"But they are factors, they do figure in my decision" laughed Amerigo as he took her into his arms.

Several days before this conversation had taken place on the waterfront. Amerigo and several pilots had joined Bishop Fonseca.

"In my voyage for Portugal I have learned that the land Columbus found is not just islands but a large new continent," stated Amerigo to the surprised group.

"What made you come to that conclusion?" asked the Bishop.

"In my last two voyages, I have traveled along about 6000 miles of unbroken coast. A coast line unbroken by any strait and the rivers that pour great quantities of fresh water into the sea could only indicate a large land mass," stated Amerigo firmly.

"An enormous amount of water certainly gushes forth from the rivers. I can vouch for that," added Vicente Yanez Pinzon. "That would put Asia much farther away," he stated.

"If I am right," Amerigo added, "none of the ancients believed there was a continent south of the equator but our voyages have proved them wrong. We also now are sure that this continent is not a part of Asia."

"Why do you say that?" inquired Juan de la Cosa.

"It is a fact that all Asia's mainland lies north of the equator. We sailed far south of it and even hundreds of miles south of the Tropic of Capricorn, and still we found unbroken coastline," stated Amerigo. "It has to be another continent and most of it lies within Spanish territory."

"Are you sure about the Line of Demarcation," asked the Bishop.

"If I am right it is 47 degrees 50 seconds west of Greenwich," stated Amerigo. "I have also come to the conclusion that a degree is considerably larger than Columbus thought. It is even larger than Ptolemy declared. My figure is not far from Toscanelli's calculations," added Amerigo.

"Instead of the 3,850 Roman miles to Cipangu that Columbus figured, I believe it to be almost 11,500," again Amerigo spoke with conviction.

"We need more proof so we can update our maps," said the Bishop.

"My map that I made in 1500 needs updating," said Juan de la Cosa.

"Another voyage must be sent out immediately to ascertain your statement and to search for the strait that will lead us to the Indian waters," stated the Bishop.

Plans for the voyage began immediately. (It should be remembered that the current estimate of the circumference of the earth is only about fifty miles more than Amerigo's estimate.)

Chapter XXVI

A Year of Confusion in Spain

It was the year 1505. This was a year of confusion in Spain. Queen Isabella's death in late 1504, had left a vacuum that would be hard to fill. She was a very able queen who was much loved and respected. She was known as "the queen on horseback" for she was most often seen by the people when riding her horse back and forth from court to court as it moved from city to city.

Dona Joanna of Castile who had inherited the throne from Isabella was in Austria at the time of her mother's death. She and her husband, Philip, who was Archduke of Austria and son of Maximilian I came immediately to Spain. Philip brought with him an escort of German soldiers and contested Ferdinand's right as regent. It was then that the state of confusion in Spain began. Spain seemed to have two Kings. Which king to obey was the big question. This put the affairs of the Board of Trade in Seville in a quandary. They sent Amerigo to court with three letters to find out whose orders to obey. The directions given to Amerigo are in the letters below:

To Captain Amerigo Vespucci:

You will take three letters for the king, for Vila, his Grand Chamberlain and his secretary, Gricio: also five memorials: one upon dispatch of armaments, two others received from Hispaniola concerning the tower that King Ferdinand ordered to be built upon the Pearl Coast, and the remaining two upon the caravels, which are in the service of Espaniola, and concerning the things necessary for the fortress that is being built there.

If Gricio is at court and is in charge of the affairs of the Indies, give him the letters, show him the memorials and he will guide you to the ear of the king and expedite the business.

We are informed, however, that perhaps the king has entrusted the business of the Indies to M de Vila, his Grand Chamberlain. If that is the case, go directly to him. What we principally desire is a full understanding of the agreement entered into between the king, Philip, our Lord, and King Ferdinand that we may give each prince that which is his.

Amerigo made his way to court and stopped to see the ailing Columbus. Columbus gave Amerigo the following letter to his son, Diego, who was then at the court. He had been a courtier there since Columbus's first memorable voyage in 1492. This letter was translated by the historian who found it. It is now preserved in Ferdinand Columbus's library, the Biblioteca Columbus, in Seville and can be seen there today.

February 5,1505

My dear son:

Diego Mendez left here Monday, the third of this month. Since his departure, I have talked with Amerigo Vespucci, who is on his way to court, where he has been called on several points connected with navigation. He has at all times shown the desire to be pleasant to me; he is an honest man. As with many others, fortune has not been kind to him. His efforts have not brought him the reward he might, by right, have expected. He is going (to the court) with a sincere desire to obtain something favorable for me, should the opportunity offer itself. From here I cannot advise him more specifically how to be of use to me, because I don't know what is expected of him; but he is decided to do all in his power on my behalf to see what can be done to advantage there, and labor for it, that he may know and speak of everything and devote himself to the word; and if everything be done in secrecy, that no suspicion may arise, I have said all I can say to him touching the business, and have informed him of all payments that have been made to me and what is due.

This letter is also for the Adelantado, that he may avail himself of any advantage and advice on the subject. His Highness believes that his ships were in the best and richest of the Indies and if he desires to know anything more, I will satisfy him with word of mouth, for it is impossible for him to tell by letter.

May our Lord have you in his holy keeping.

Done at Seville February 5, 1505

Thy father who loves you better than
himself,

Christopher Columbus

S

S A S

X M Y

Y P O   F E R N S

(above - Columbus's strange signature)

The above letter was delivered to Diego and it shows that Columbus and Amerigo were friends.

When Amerigo arrived at court, he found that King Ferdinand had hastily left for his kingdom in Naples. His recent marriage to Germaine de Foix, the niece of the king of France, so soon after Isabella's death, had infuriated the people of Castile so that he was forced to step aside and leave Philip in charge.

Amerigo delivered to Philip the letter from the Board of Trade. He received permission from Philip for a voyage of exploration to the River del Plata in South America. Also in the name of Queen Joanna Philip made Amerigo a Spanish citizen.

This was in August 1505. Whether Philip and Joanna would have helped Columbus is not known and the expedition to the Rio del Plata never sailed, for Philip died unexpectedly in September 1505. Vicente Yanez Pinzon and Amerigo were scheduled to sail on this voyage and it may have been the voyage that the historian, Herrera, in his history written in the early 1600's, confused with the 1497 voyage of Pinzon and Amerigo. It may have been this voyage that Ralph Waldo Emerson referred to in his famous quotation as "the expedition that never sailed." Emerson's quotation in the middle of the 19th century seems to have colored all mention of Amerigo in American school books.

The actual facts about Philip's death remain in doubt. The palace records show that after a strenuous game of tennis, he drank a pitcher of ice cold lemonade and died of heart failure. It was rumored, however, that he was poisoned by order, by Mosen Ferrer, a gentleman of the bed chamber.

Queen Joanna was over come with grief by her husband's death. She was taken to a nearby palace in a state of madness. She was to remain there the rest of her life.

The affairs of the Board of Trade were again in a state of confusion. All was postponed until Fredinand could return from Naples. It was the Archbishop of Toledo Jimenez who held Castile with a firm hand until he returned. Ferdinand, then, became the undisputed ruler of Spain under the "nominal regency" of his daughter Queen Joanna.

Chapter XXVII

The Death of Columbus

It was the year 1506. This was the year Columbus died. Columbus was in a weakened condition after returning from his high voyage. For a time he lived in a rented house in Seville. It was at this house that he was visited by Amerigo when Amerigo was on his way to court. Columbus remembered Queen Joanna when she was just a child playing in the courtyard. She was friendly to him then. He sent the letter to the court hoping that she would help him now, but after Philip's death and her madness, he gave up hope.

Both of his sons were at the court, Ferdinand, the younger one, had returned to his job there as a Page after the Fourth Voyage and had received all his back pay. Diego, the older son, was still at the court. He had been there since his fathers first great voyage and now was a valued courtier. He soon would marry into the Royal Family. When Columbus recovered enough to travel he also went to the court and followed it as it moved from Salamanca to Valladolid. He no longer hoped to be returned as governor to Hispaniola but he was petitioning for what he believed was his just due. King Ferdinand proposed appointing an arbitrator to settle his claim against the crown. Columbus refused this offer just as he had refused the offer of a grand estate "with a large rent roll".

At Valladolid, Columbus took a turn for the worse. He again took up residence in a rented home and revised his will. He provided that a house in Genoa be kept open perpetually for his descendants and that a chapel be built in Hispaniola so that daily masses might be said for his immortal soul. He made his son, Diego, his heir but commanded him to provide for Beatriz, the mother of Ferdinand, and also for Ferdinand. Columbus died on May 20, 1506.

According to Columbus's biographer, Samuel Eliot Morison, he was far from penniless when he died. His share of the gold from his Fourth Voyage was considerable. Carvajal had also brought back a large sum in the ship that rode out the storm. Ovando, when Columbus had finally reached Santo Domingo in 1504, delivered to him his share of the recently mined gold which filled a chest. He continued to receive 2% of the gold found in the new world instead of the 10% that he thought was his due, but even with the two percent, Columbus was a rich man according to the standards of the day, and left his sons well off. Also many of the promises made to him by the sovereigns were kept.

Three years after his father's death Diego was made governor of Hispaniola. He had married a lady of royal blood, the princess, Dona Maria de Toledo. She was a kinswoman of King Ferdinand for her paternal grandmother was a sister of Ferdinand's mother. Diego proved to be a more able governor than his father had been. While in Hispaniola he built the governor's mansion and the cathedral that his father had planned, the ruins of which may still be seen in Santo Domingo.

Columbus's younger son, Ferdinand, went to Hispaniola with his brother but such a life did not appeal to him. He returned to Spain and became a scholar and humanist. He traveled all over Europe and collected a large library of books which today can be seen in Seville. It is known as the Biblioteca Columbus and contains many of Columbus's letters and writings. Ferdinand also wrote a biography of his famous father.

Ferdinand and Diego buried their father in the church of San Francisco de la Santa Maria de la Antigus in Valladolid. No notable persons from the Royal Court were sent to attend his funeral. He died before Balboa discovered the Pacific Ocean and before Magellan's famous voyage. He died before Cortez conquered Mexico and before Pizarro entered Peru, and even before Ponce de Leon explored Florida. He had the misfortune of dying before the world realized the enormous importance of his discovery.

Three years after Columbus's death, his body by order of his son, Diego, was moved to the La Cuevas Monastery Chapel in Triana across the Quadalquiver River From Seville. Both of Columbus's brothers, Bartholomew and Don Diego were later buried there. This monastery was secularized in the 19th century and is now a part of the tile factory of Triana. It was in this monastery that Columbus had spent much of his time between his voyages. His first resting place, the Church of San Francisco was later made into a Columbus Museum.

After the Cathedral of Santo Domingo was built in Santa Domingo again Columbus's body was moved there and it was placed on the High Altar of the Cathedral.

In 1795, when Santo Domingo was ceded to France by the Treaty of Basil, the body of Columbus was again moved, this time to the High Altar of the Cathedral of Havana, Cuba. Here it remained until early 1800 when Cuba became independent. Columbus's remains were then moved from Havana and are now resting in the great Cathedral of Seville.

This still does not complete the story of the remains of Columbus for when in 1877, the Santo Domingo Cathedral was being repaired two boxes or lead caskets badly "ravished by time" were found. On one box was inscribed Don Luis Colon, the grandson of the first Admiral. On the other was "The illustrious and excellent man, Don Cristobal Colon. Could this have been the lead casket removed from Triana so many years before? Probably not but some of the ashes from it fell to the floor when the small box was moved. They were taken to four cities, Genoa, Rome, Pavia, and New York. Even Columbus's body in death like in life has been restless.

It is interesting that descendants of Columbus are alive today and still bear the title Admiral of the Ocean Sea. Diego's son, Luis inherited the title and was governor of Hispaniola, but he did not inherit Diego's ability. He married the Marquess of Jamaica and his title was Duke of Veragua with a pension of 10,000 ducats. Later he was made Duke of Vega also with an extra pension of 7,000 ducats. He ruled Hispaniola until 1551. He died in 1572 and left a daughter. Her son, Nuno Colon de Portugal, was the great grandson of Columbus. Nuno great grand daughter was Catalina Venturo. She married a Scotchman, Fitz James Stuart, son of Duke of Berwick and a grandson of James II of England and of Arabella Churchill.

The twentieth century descendant of Columbus is Cristobal Colon de Carvajal y Marata, Hurtado de Mendoza y Perez del Pulgar, and Admiral of the Ocean Sea. He was born in 1925, and "styles himself as the 17th Duke of Veragua and 15th Duke of Vega, also Marquess of Jamaica." He wears an Admiral's uniform on ceremonial occasions.

Another 20th century descendant of Columbus is Rafael Meto y Corladellas who has produced an heir.

So Columbus's name and fame lives on even if the New World was not named for him. Almost every state in the United States has a city named for Columbus. In South America the country, Columbia, is named for him and Canada has a province, British Columbia.

Hundreds and perhaps thousands of statues honor him, probably the most famous is in the harbor at Barcelona. The prestigious Columbia University in New York City also honors him with his name. The United States government has set aside October 12th the date of his famous landing, as a national holiday. It is sad that he died before the world realized the immense importance of his discovery.

Chapter XXVIII

America: The Origin of the Name

It was the year 1507. This was the year the word AMERICA was coined and put on a map for the first time. The origin of the word was the work of a group of young and talented scholars who had just acquired a printing press. They had come together in a monastery in the small town of Saint-Die, high in the Vosges Mountains in northeastern France. With this printing press and under the sponsorship of Rene, the ruling duke of the province, they had lofty plans. They, inspired by the revival of learning and art which was gradually coming over the Alps from Italy, resolved to teach and spread knowledge by printing famous books. Their first famous book would be a revised version of Ptolemy's geography, which until that time had been considered by scholars "unsurpassable and complete". Now, because of the recent voyages by the Portuguese and Spanish, it needed updating. In their research they found that Portuguese mariners had rounded the African continent and had succeeded in finding a water route to the Indies. They knew that it was the Portuguese, Bartholomew Diaz in 1486, who first navigated the treacherous waters off the Cape of Good Hope. Vasco de Gama, also a Portuguese, had in 1497 followed him and had been the first to reach the Indies by a water route. They also knew of Cabral's successful voyage to India that returned with much rich cargo.

These young scholars also knew about Columbus's famous voyage across the great Ocean Sea. They also knew that he had not found any of the riches of the Orient.

They knew, also, about the voyages of John and Sebastian Cabot to Newfoundland and along the North American coast. All this they planned to put in their geography but Amerigo's letters announcing the news of a new continent, a fourth part of the world excited them more.

These young scholars without hesitation put aside for a time the revision of Ptolemy's work and produced and printed a little booklet using the information in Amerigo's Mundus Novus and Soderini letters. They gave it the title <u>Cosmographiae Introdutio</u>. It had only one hundred three pages. In it they made a quick summary of the known principles of geography but most of it was about the discovery of a new continent, a fourth part of the world. The Soderini letter was included for it gave so much interesting information about the people, plants and animals of the new land. They printed it in full and to honor their patron, Rene, they addressed the letter as if it had been written to him by Amerigo. This change added to confusion about the origin of the name America because Amerigo never knew Rene. This little booklet was widely read in Europe and edition after edition was printed and circulated.

To accompany this booklet Martin Waldseemuller, one of the young scholars and a skilled cartographer, made a map of the new lands. The map is described as being a beautiful work of cartography and design. On this map he painted two portraits, one of Ptolemy and one of Amerigo Vespucci, Ptolemy facing east and Amerigo facing west. On the map both the north and south continents were connected by an isthmus. The outline of the Southern continent was surprisingly correct as was the outline of the Gulf of Mexico. Both were based on Amerigo's sketches.

To introduce the <u>Cosmographiae Introdutio</u>, Matthias Ringman, the poet in this group of young scholars wrote the following lines:

A land exist unknown on your
map, Ptolemy
Situated between the Tropic of Cancer
and rainy Aquarius
Surrounded by the vast sea.
In this land
ablaze with light dwell many
naked people.
A king in whom Portugal takes great pride
discovered it
Sending a fleet across the stormy sea.
What more shall I say,
The lands and customs of these people,
Here in this book you will learn.
by Ringman

Matthias Ringman is believed to be the one who coined the word AMERICA. Other important members of this group were Vautrin Lud, who purchased the printing press, and Nicholas Lud, his nephew and the printer, and an author, Jean Basin, who had just finished a treatise on the art of eloquent speech. They were a distinguished group.

Waldseemuller, to introduce the word AMERICA on his map, wrote the following statement:

> But now these parts have been extensively explored, and another part of the world has been discovered by Amerigo Vespucci, wherefore, I do not see what is rightly to hinder us from calling it AMERIGE [GE from Greek meaning land of], i.e., the land of Amerigo or AMERICA, its discoverer . . .

Later, in 1511, another edition of this map was printed. On it the name America was left off, possibly because Waldseemuller realized that Columbus was the discoverer. By that time the word was so well known and it went so well with the names Europe, Asia, and Africa, it was too late. Other map makers used it. The word according to Stefan Zweig, the author of Amerigo, A Comedy Of Errors In History, wrote that the word AMERICA "took on a life of its own . . . it was a conquering word . . . imperiously it thrust aside all other names . . . .." The word had power and so did the fledgling printing press, which then was only fifty years old. The word AMERICA had been printed and so widely accepted that it could not be recalled and at that time no one objected to the name.

More years passed. Cortez conquered Mexico, Pizarro conquered Peru, and De Soto explored the southeastern part of North America. Finally the importance of Columbus's discovery was realized and the big question "What has Columbus discovered?" was answered. He had discovered another hemisphere with two large continents.

In Spain, after Columbus's death the new land continued to be called the Indies, the name Columbus had given to it. Little attention was given to America's name on the southern continent, but in 1538, when Mercator published his great map, with the name AMERICA on both continents, Spain became concerned. Another big question arose:

Why were both North America and South America named for Amerigo and not for Columbus?

Bartolome de las Casas, the first great historian of the period, was just writing his history of the early explorations. He protested and without knowing the origin of the word AMERICA jumped to the conclusion that South America was named for Amerigo because he falsely claimed to be the first to touch the mainland of that continent. (A claim that Amerigo never made.)

Las Casas's history was not published until fifty years after his death because of a provision in his will. This manuscript was lost and later found and published by the historian, Herrera, in 1601. Herrera and many later historians wrote that Amerigo had falsely claimed to be the discoverer of the New World. He and others not finding any record of the secret voyage claimed that it never sailed.

Other historians more careful in their research, went through the many commercial papers and maps of the period, and found no evidence that Amerigo had claimed to be the discoverer. They did find that he made long voyages along the coast of South America and North America and that he held the office of pilot-major. They wrote in defense of Amerigo. A bitter controversy arose and lingers until this day. In early American history textbooks, it was written that Amerigo usurped the name from Columbus and even after the origin of the name was known only a scant paragraph is devoted to him.

Why was there so much confusion about the naming of AMERICA? The group of young scholars in Saint-Die soon parted. Matthias Ringman died in 1514, Waldseemuller in 1518, and his map disappeared. Another famous map, the La Cosa map of 1500, showing the earliest explorations also disappeared. These maps give strong evidence that the 1497 voyage was made for on them are many of the names given by Amerigo.

These maps probably were hidden because the kings made it illegal to print any map of new discoveries and they feared the Inquisition since the church also denied the existence of a fourth continent. Amerigo's letters too, were buried in the archives of Florence and were forgotten.

The origin of the word was finally unearthed by Alexander von Humboldt (1769-1859), the great German scientist, explorer, and naturalist but not until the middle of the nineteenth century. He found the Saint-Die story while he was living in Paris writing his great Geographie du Noveau. His findings proved that Amerigo Vespucci had no part in the naming of the new continent but that the name AMERICA originated in a hidden spot in the Vosges Mountains of France. He found that the name was put on Waldseemuller's map without Amerigo's knowledge or consent.

Humboldt also found the original Juan de la Cosa map (1500) in 1832, in the library of Baron Walcknaer long after the Baron's death. He bought the map at an auction in Paris for the Queen of Spain. It is now in the Naval Museum in Madrid. Waldseemuller's map remained lost until 1900. It was found by Professor Fisher in the library at Wolfegg Castle in Germany. It is now in the Lenox Collection in the New York Library. Amerigo's letters have one by one been found. They also shed light on the controversial question, "Why were the Americas named for Amerigo and not for Columbus?"

The origin of the name is now known but the controversy continues possibly because of the words of a few of America's famous authors, Ralph Waldo Emerson, Washington Irving, and William Hickling Prescott. Irving was the earliest to write critically of Amerigo. He had been ambassador to Spain and he had great sympathy for Columbus. He wrote stressing Columbus's poverty, his chains and his neglect by the crown. Prescott and Emerson followed his lead and today even though it has been proven that Amerigo had no part in the naming of America, modern history books continue to write very little about Amerigo. Possibly because of these words of Emerson maligning Amerigo:

> Strange . . . that broad America must wear the name of a thief. Amerigo Vespucci, the pickle dealer at Seville . . . . whose highest navel rank was boatswain's mate in an expedition that never sailed, managed in this lying world, to supplant Columbus and baptize half the earth with his own name.

"In these words," writes Daniel J. Boorstin, "There is not a word of truth." Boorstin further states that Emerson, in his writings was often careless of his facts. Who is Daniel J. Boorstin who dares to write criticizing our great author? He was for five years the Preston and Sterling Morton Distinguished Service Professor of American History at the University of Chicago, he was the director of the National Museum of History and Technology, Senior historian of the Smithsonian Institution, Washington, D. C., and the Librarian of Congress since 1975. He was a Rhodes Scholar and has been a visiting professor of American History at many universities abroad. He is certainly one of American's greatest historians.

Boorstin in 1983, published a great and fascinating history titled, The Discoverers, a History of Man's Search to Know the World and Himself. In this history he devotes two chapters to Christopher Columbus and one full chapter to Amerigo Vespucci.

Boorstin's does not write about the usual battles, empires, and political leaders but about the great beginnings and the great discoveries. He writes about "the human quest for what man does not know." His heroes "Are men with an insatiable hunger for knowledge and the courage to venture into the unknown." Among his heroes are Ptolemy, Marco Polo, Copernicus, Kepler, Galileo, Columbus, Amerigo and many others. It is they that he writes about in his distinguished work The Discoverers. They are, he believes, the truly remarkable figures in history.

Chapter XXIX

Ferdinand Appoints Amerigo Pilot-Major

It was the year 1508. Ferdinand with the aid of Jimenez, the Archbishop of Toledo, again assumed the complete control of Spain. He ruled as regent under the nominal regency of his daughter, Queen Joanna, and would continue to be in control until his death early in 1516. The continuing information about the great land to the west had gradually made him realize the great importance of Columbus's discovery. He was now ready to make serious plans. He sent for Juan de la Cosa, Juan Diaz la Solis, Vicente Yanez Pinzon, and Amerigo Vespucci. They were the best known maritime navigators in Spain.

In 1508, the problem with Portugal was being diplomatically settled and plans were again underway for the Pinzon and Amerigo voyage south to the mouth of the La Plata River to seek a strait around the continent They fully expected it would lead to the Indies. At this meeting, plans were to change. Pinzon and Solis were to command this important voyage. Amerigo was appointed to the new position of pilot-major of Spain. Juan de la Cosa was appointed Alguazil mayor or governor of the province to be organized at the Gulf of Darien.

Alonso de Ojeda who had been successful in subduing the Indians in Hispaniola and who in 1499, was in charge of the second voyage of Amerigo, was to share in the rule of the northern part of that province.

Up to the time of Columbus's great discovery, Spain had little interest in maritime affairs. Now as more and more voyages had been made and more and more land was being discovered, it became the prime interest of Spain and would continue to be for three centuries. The appointment of a pilot-major was the first of many steps made to make ocean travel safer and more profitable. The two primary duties of the pilot-major were to train pilots and to prepare and update maps for the pilots.

Ferdinand decreed that "all pilots and all seaman who wanted to be pilots be trained in the use of the quadrant and the use of the astrolabe so they might make use of them on their voyages . . . and without this knowledge they may not sail on any Spanish ships as pilots, nor secure a salary for pilotage, nor could any merchant engage them as pilots, nor shipmasters take them aboard unless they have been examined by you, Amerigo Vespucci, and receive from you a certificate of examination . . . .."

King Ferdinand also gave the following orders concerning charts and maps:

"There are many general charts drawn up by different ship masters depicting and indicating the lands and islands of the Indies of our possessions . . . which vary greatly one from another. To establish consensus and unity the king decides that there should be one general chart showing each point of land, each island, each river mouth, each bay in its proper location. We order our officials of the Seville Trade Board for the Indies to bring together the most skilled of all our pilots who may be ashore at the time, and in the presence of you, Amerigo Vespucci, our pilot-major, to settle upon and draw up a master map of all the lands and islands of the Indies discovered up to this moment belonging to our kingdom and realms and on the basis of their opinion and discussion and on the decision taken by you, our aforesaid pilot-major, a master chart be drawn up to be known as The Royal Chart, by which all pilots are to govern and guide themselves."

It was further decreed that no chart other than those drawn up by Amerigo Vespucci were to be used "under penalty of a fifty doubloon fine" and that any pilot finding anything not on the master chart was to go to Amerigo's school and report it.

In order that no one be ignorant of the law, it was ordered that the people be called together by the town crier to the sound of drums, and the Royal Letter be publicly read.

The king's order was carried out in all towns, cities, and hamlets of Spain. Amerigo's name was widely broadcast but spelled in various ways; Espuchi, Despuchi, Espuche, or Bespuchie. No wonder in Spain he was always known simply as Amerigo.

The four pilots after the important decision of March 22, 1508, hurried back to Seville. Pinzon and Solis would prepare for the big voyage to the La Plate River; Juan de la Cosa soon left for the Pearl Coast and then to the Gulf of Darien; Amerigo immediately began to set up his school for pilots. They had wanted such action from the king and were anxious to carry out his orders.

Pinzon and Solis's hoping to finding a strait near the La Plata River sailed June 29, 1508. This voyage proved to be a disappointment. No strait was found, the ship only reached latitude 40 degrees south. A disagreement between the two leaders caused them to abandon the search. They returned to Seville in October of 1509. It would be six years later and after Amerigo's death before another voyage would be made to the La Plata.

In the meantime in Seville, Maria, Luisa, and Pedro were dining at the Sierpes Cafe. They expected Amerigo's return and left word for him to join them.

"It will be interesting to find out what King Ferdinand's plans are for Spain. The news of a new continent south of the equator and the other explorations are too important to be ignored," said Pedro. "I feel sure he will now okay the voyage to go south of the equator."

"And that will mean Amerigo will be gone another two years," sighed Maria. "I had so hoped that by this time he would have had enough of the sea and would continue his business in Seville."

"We had all hoped so," agreed Luisa, "but he is still hoping to find Ptolemy's Strait of Catigara."

Just at that moment, Amerigo entered the cafe, "There he is," cried Maria.

"What great news do you bring?" quickly asked Pedro.

"It is indeed great news," laughed Amerigo, "but quite different from what I expected."

"Are the plans for the big voyage still on," asked Maria anxiously.

"Yes," responded Amerigo, "but that is not the biggest news."

"Tell us," Maria spoke quickly.

"You, Maria," said Amerigo, "are now the wife of the newly appointed Pilot-Major of Spain."

"What?" exclaimed the astonished three. "What is a pilot-major?"

"It will be my duty to train all pilots and all those who want to be pilots in the use of the quadrant and astrolabe. Each will be required to study navigation and will be required to stand an examination before getting a license as pilots. I will be a teacher, and establish a school," finished Amerigo.

"What about plans for the big voyage?" questioned Pedro, "Surely that will go on."

"Yes," said Amerigo, "King Ferdinand has ordered Vicente Yanez Pinzon and Juan de la Solis to make that voyage. Both are excellent pilots."

"Then you will not be going to sea again?" hopefully questioned Maria.

"No, at least not for now. I will be busy establishing the school," answered Amerigo.

"Well, that is a relief," stated Maria. "I guess I will have to thank King Ferdinand for making my wish come true."

"And if you agree to it, I will establish the school in the west wing of your villa?" asked Amerigo.

"Then you will even work at home," said Maria gaily. "That will suit me fine."

"But where are Giovanni and Elena. I want to tell them the news," said Amerigo.

"They will join us soon," laughed Maria. "Now they are off dancing with the young folks."

"I want Giovanni to be my assistant and help me in the map making. He has learned well not only the art of sailing but is showing talent in map making," said Amerigo.

Later that evening Amerigo wrote the following letter to Giorgio.

To my dear uncle, Giorgio Antonio Vespucci,

You will be surprised and I hope pleased to learn that I am now to become a teacher, a teacher like you, my beloved uncle. On March 22, 1508, King Ferdinand called a meeting of the navigators of Spain. He is now seeking to organize the navigation of Spain much as it has been done in Portugal. He has decreed that all pilots be trained and he has chosen me to be the teacher. I will organize a school, train all pilots in the use of the quadrant, the astrolabe, and in astronomy. My title will be Pilot-Major of Spain. It will be a big undertaking but I welcome the opportunity. I just hope I can instill in my pilot pupils the same enthusiasm you gave to me and your other pupils.

And another bit of news that will please both you and my brother, Antonio. I will chose Giovanni as my assistant. He has learned much of what I know. I taught him during the long nights at sea and he has been an apt pupil. He also shows great talent in map making. One of my tasks as pilot-major is to bring together all the pilots with their maps and charts and make a master chart to be known as the Royal Chart. It will be a living map. All new lands, islands, bays, and rivers will be recorded as soon as they have been discovered. It is an exciting mission and I'm proud to have been chosen.

No, doubt, it is to you that I owe the honor for it was you who taught and inspired me to seek knowledge. Thank you so much.

I, also, during the few months spent in Lisbon learned much about King Emanuel's naval organization. That knowledge will be of much help for up until this time Spain has had practically no such organization. I will have to begin anew.

And, too, I want you to know of Maria's part. She has even taught me for as you know both her father and first husband were seaman, and she listened to them and often when Giovanni and I were discussing navigation, she would tell us what they thought about the subject. Her biggest help, though, has been in allowing me the freedom to go, to see and to learn. There were many times that I felt guilty about leaving her for such long periods of time. She, however, was ever supportive and always seemed interested in knowing my plans and my hopes. That doesn't mean that she never complained but when she did it was in a teasing fashion.

I realize now, why you encouraged me to find a wife. I remember that you said that the relationship between a man and his wife was one you, being a monk, could never experience. You went on to say it was possibly the relationship in life you missed most. I want you to know that I have found the happiness you hoped I would find. The fact that I have realized it and cherished it, is because of that conversation with you. I have much to thank you for Uncle Giorgio

Giorgio, you must be now close to eighty. You have used your years well and I hope I can be remembered as a great teacher just as you are. My happiness would be complete if you would come to Seville to be with us.

With my regards to the family,

Much love,

Your grateful nephew,

Amerigo, Pilot-Major of Spain

Chapter XXX

The Discovery of America: The Third Decade

It was the year 1512. This was the year Amerigo Vespucci died. Two decades had passed since Columbus's great discovery. Many more voyages to the new land had been made and even more would be made before the full extent and value of that voyage would be realized. Many of the early explorers and discoveries would depart this world during this third decade, leaving guideposts for the next generation.

Queen Isabella had died in 1504, and Columbus, two years later in 1506. They were the first two players in this great drama. Juan de la Cosa, the great navigator and map maker died in 1510. He and Alonso de la Ojeda, soon after being appointed joint governors of the Gulf of Darien by King Ferdinand, left to organize a colony there. Ojeda, ever the impulsive one, incurred the anger of the natives and both he and La Cosa were shot in a skirmish with poisoned arrows. La Cosa died but Ojeda, again, showed his resourcefulness. He ordered one of his men to burn out his wound with a red-hot iron. He survived but he never became a successful administrator of his colony. Without the steadying hand of Juan de Cosa, he soon had to flee to Puerto Rico, but there also ran into trouble. He died in Hispaniola in 1515, a poor and broken man.

Juan de la Solis followed Amerigo as pilot-major of Spain. In 1516, while still pilot-major he headed an expedition to the mouth of the River de la Plata still searching for the ever elusive strait that would lead to the great ocean, the one discovered three years earlier by Balboa. With his ships anchored well off-shore, de la Solis and a few unarmed men rowed ashore to confer with what they thought were friendly Indians. The Indians, instead of being friendly, pounced upon these unsuspecting men, captured them, and according to legend, they were quartered, barbecued, and eaten by the savages. Their helpless shipmates out of range of gun fire looked on in horror. They then, without their leader, quickly hastened back to Spain. The mouth of the great Rio de la Plata was still to be explored. For a while, however, this river was known as Rio de la Solis.

The last days of Vicente Yanez Pinzon are not known but he did go to Puerto Rico. He probably died there in 1518 and did not live to know that the whole Pinzon family was ennobled by Charles V in 1519. He did live long enough to testify in the Probansas, the famous law suit filed against the crown by Diego, the son of Columbus. This suit lasted from 1508 to 1515, and was very thorough. At the close of the case, Diego retained the title Admiral of the Ocean Sea, was awarded two percent of the gold found, and was appointed governor of Hispaniola. It is interesting to note that no word in this trial was uttered against Amerigo accusing him of usurping the name from Columbus. Ferdinand Columbus had in his possession a copy of Waldseemuller's map, on which was printed the name America, but he never in his life time said a word against Amerigo. The name America on that map was only on the part today known as Brazil. It was not until 1538, when Geradus Kaufman (Mercator) published his famous projection map that the name AMERICA was given to both the north and south continents.

King Ferdinand's death occurred in 1516, leaving the throne to his grandson, Charles of Austria, who would be known as Charles V. He became the first and greatest of all the Hapsburg rulers. He ruled Spain from 1516 to 1556. Then he abdicated the throne to his son Philip II, and retired to a monastery where he died in 1558. It was Charles V who gave Magellan the permission to make his round-the-world voyage after the King of Portugal had refused to do so. He like his grandmother, Queen Isabella, was able to look into the future and thus Spain sponsored the two greatest voyages of all time.

Amerigo's last days were happy and satisfying for him and for his wife, Maria. They worked together to set up the school for pilots and to create the master charts for King Ferdinand. Amerigo only was to live four years more for he had contracted malaria during his voyages. He died quietly in his home in Seville in 1512. His body was embalmed and taken to Florence and buried in the d'Oqnissanti Chapel as was his Vespucci ancestors.

Juan de la Solis and Sebastian Cabot, who were to follow Amerigo as pilot-major were commanded to give Maria Cerezo a generous portion of their salary as a pension, perhaps because the school continued to be conducted from her villa and the new pilot-majors used Amerigo's maps and charts. Maria continued to receive this pension until her death.

Amerigo's nephew, Giovanni Vespucci, was his uncle's assistant while he was pilot-major and became the official map maker of Spain. He, too, later would hold the office of pilot-major and he, like his uncle, would become a Spanish citizen. His name Giovanni was changed to the Spanish, Juan Vespucci. One of his maps is still extant and is, along with a copy of Waldseemuller's map of 1507, in the rare book division of the New York Public Library.

At that time many of the early maps and charts were guarded jealously by the kings of Spain and Portugal. All were declared to be the property of the state. For this reason the maps and charts of Amerigo were not signed and many were lost. Although sixty editions of Amerigo's letters were printed and widely read in Europe, none were ever printed in Spain partly because of fear of the Inquisition and partly because the importance of the newly discovered continent was not realized, even by Amerigo, himself. He, along with the king, with Columbus, and others were still intent on finding a water route to the Indies. The continent then seemed mainly a hinderance to their objective. The riches of the Orient blinded them.

The excitement in Europe caused by Amerigo's announcement of the discovery of a new continent was soon silenced by fear of the Inquisition. The rising movement of the great Reformation in the church brought about a new resurgence of Catholicism in Europe. Ptolemy's maps were being reprinted on the new printing press and his map showed only three continents; Europe, Asia, and Africa. The church had adopted Ptolemy's geography as the absolute truth for three continents surrounded by one great Ocean Sea carried out the theme of the Holy Trinity, three in one. "Any variation of Ptolemy's views was suspect." His findings were considered by the church as "the final word" and became almost canonical. Even the great map maker, Mercator, because of his views was arrested and held for four months before being released. He then moved to Italy where the church was more tolerant. It was not until Magellan's ship finally returned to Spain and Cortez and Pizarro were pouring gold into the Spanish treasury that Europe turned seriously to the colonization of the Americas and Mercator dared to publish his map showing both of the continents in the New World. On his famous map Mercator gave the name AMERICA to the northern continent as well as to the southern one. This fixed the name for all time. All map makers followed him. Amerigo and Columbus had been dead for almost thirty years when Mercator published his map in 1538.

While Amerigo has been largely ignored by American history, his accomplishments were many. To summaries them, he was the first to declare that South America was a new continent and not a part of Asia. He was the first to put forth the concept that another ocean must be crossed before Asia could be reached. He evolved a system of computing nearly perfect longitude by his study of the heavenly bodies, and thus was able to estimate the earth circumference within fifty miles of the modern figure. He explored six thousand miles of the coast of South America and called attention to the equatorial ocean currents and was the first to cross the equator in the new hemisphere. He was probably the first along with his shipmates to see the great Amazon River, and the Rio de la Plata. Amerigo accounts of his voyage contributed much to the European knowledge of the New World. He was the first navigator besides Columbus that knew how to write well. It is, however, according to the Columbia Encyclopedia, "The scientific application of his discoveries that make his achievements remarkable." As his god parents had predicted, he became a great teacher of pilots, and his native Florence honored him as a worthy citizen by having the Vespucci house lighted for three nights. In his birthplace a stone was erected in his honor inscribed as follows:

In this little village of Peretola the noble and powerful family of the Vespucci had its orgin, one of whos sons was the great Amerigo from whom America got its name.

Today in Florence Amerigo's statue stands tall and his head is carved in the facade along with the heads of Toscanelli, Galileo, Ficini, and Columbus in the great cathedral of Santa Maria del Fiore.

Underneath is this quotation from Dante:

The way I pass ne'er yet was run.

THE END

Epilogue

Christopher Columbus was the first to sail into the unknown. He discovered a vast new land. "I have found a water route to the Indies," he announced, but years passed and no one was sure what he had discovered.

Amerigo Vespucci followed Columbus and after sailing six thousand miles along the shore of South America announced, "I have found a new continent, a fourth part of the world, another hemisphere. He gave meaning and understanding to Columbus's great discovery.

The new land was named for Amerigo Vespucci soon after he announced the exciting news that a fourth part of the world had been discovered. Two young scholars, Waldseemuller and Ringman, coined the word AMERICA and put it on a map. Other names were considered but the word America prevailed, even after the importance of Columbus's discovery was realized. It was a beautiful word for this "land not ruled by kings or tyrants". These words written by Amerigo describing the New World made a lasting imprint on the many oppressed Europeans, and thousands seeking freedom followed Columbus into the unknown. They peopled the new land of America and have for five hundred years kept it the land of the free.

Bibliography

Adams, Edward Dean, <u>America and the Americans The
　　Name and Its Significance,</u> Privately printed by
　　Bartlett Orr Press, New York, 1926, Available
　　at Murray State Univ., Murray, Ky.
Arciniegas, German, <u>Amerigo and the New World, The
　　Life and Times of Amerigo Vespucci</u>, Alfred A.
　　Knopf, New York, 1955, Available at Agnes Scott
　　Library, Atlanta and Sarasota Public Library.
Blue Guide: <u>Spain, The Mainland.</u>
Boorstin, Daniel J., <u>The Discoverers</u>, Random House,
　　New York, 1983.
Brebner, John Bartlett, <u>Explorers of North America</u>,
　　A, and C. Black, 4,5,6 Soho Square Ltd., London,
　　1923.
Brion, Marcel, <u>The Medici, A Great Florentine
　　Family</u>, Crown Publishing Co., New York, 1969.
Encyclopedias
　　　　<u>Americana</u>
　　　　<u>Britannica</u>
　　　　<u>Colliers</u>
　　　　<u>Columbia</u>

Encyclopedia of World History, McGraw.

Fisk, John, The Discovery of America, Vol II,
Houghton Miffin Company, Boston-New York, 1982.

Herriman, Paul, The Great Age of Discovery, Harper
and Bros, New York, 1958.

Hibbert, Christopher, The House of the Medici, Its
Rise and Fall, William Morrow and Co. Inc., New
York, 1978.

Kilety, Bernardine, Masters of Painting, Doubleday and Co. Inc.,
Garden City, N.J., 1964.

Lester, Charles Edward and Foster, Andrew, The Life
and Voyages of Americus Vespuccius, Baker and
Scribner, New York, 1846, Available at the
Atlanta Public Library.

Lloyd, Alan, The Spanish Centuries, Doubleday and
Company, Inc., Garden City, N. J., 1968.

Michener, James, Iberia,

Morison, Samuel Eliot, The European Discovery of
America, The Southern Voyages, Oxford Press, New
York, 1974.

Morison Samuel Eliot, Christopher Columbus, Mariner,
Little Brown and Company, Boston-Toronto, 1955.

Pohl, Julius Fredrick, Amerigo Vespucci, Pilot-
Major, Columbia University Press, New York,
1944, Available a Queens University Library,
Kingston, Ontario and Georgia Tech Library,
Atlanta.

Plumb, J. H., The Renaissance, The Heritage
Publishing Co., New York, 1958.

Rienits, Rex and Thea, The Voyages of Columbus,
Hamlyn Publishing Group, Ltd., London, New York,
Sidney, Toronto, 1970.

Winsor, Justin, Christopher Columbus, Houghton

Miffin Co., Boston, New York, 1952.

Wallbank and Taylor, <u>Civilization, Past and Present</u>,
Scott Foresman and Co., New York.

Zweig, Stefan, <u>Amerigo, A Comedy of Errors in
History</u>, Viking Press, New York, 1942,
Available at Flint River Regional Library
Griffin, Georgia.

Asia

Nor
A

– Equator –

The Wor

Australia

Miles

0   250